After reading Dr. Laura Lustig's manuscript, "Attics," I was impressed and moved by the intensity of the emotions and the vivid description of the struggle a mother is facing taking care of a disabled child.

When a baby does not respond when you expect the child to communicate and when people's reactions varied from detached to patronizing, it is no wonder that intense emotions flood the mothers' psyche. I believe that it is of great importance for any parent who has a child with disabilities to read and study this unusual book.

I was especially focused on chapter 14, "Reflections." It touched me deeply and made me admire Dr. Lustig's ability to so vividly describe her turmoil and readiness to become a super mom.

I recommend this book highly not only to parents of handicapped children but also to educators who devote their professional life to help these suffering children.

—Leon Tec, M.D., LFAPA
Psychiatrist and Child Psychiatrist
Author of: The Fear of Success; Targets; Adventure and Destiny

◆   ◆   ◆

Laura Lustig recounts the compelling journey she and her son have traveled. Jesse, now in his 40's has a disability. Written 20 years ago, her story is as relevant now as it was when it was written. As a compassionate and energetic mother, she negotiated educational, vocational, and social barriers for her son. She traveled a road of challenges, often fighting for opportunity and justice for Jesse, but also for other families confronted by childhood disability. Her story is a tale of a dedicated parent who stood up to the travails of coping with a son who has a disability, professional ignorance, and limited social opportunity. Parents will profit from Laura Lustig's courageous journey.

—Milton Seligman, Ph.D.
Professor Emeritus, University of Pittsburgh
Author of the 2007, 3rd edition of Ordinary Families, Special
Children (Guilford Pub.) (with Rosalyn Darling).

ATTICS OF
THE MIND

ATTICS OF THE MIND

✦

The Story of a Mother and her Special Son

Laura Lustig

iUniverse, Inc.
New York Lincoln Shanghai

ATTICS OF THE MIND
The Story of a Mother and her Special Son

iUniverse books may be ordered through booksellers or by contacting:

iUniverse
2021 Pine Lake Road, Suite 100
Lincoln, NE 68512
www.iuniverse.com
1-800-Authors (1-800-288-4677)

Because of the dynamic nature of the Internet, any Web addresses or links contained in this book may have changed since publication and may no longer be valid.

The views expressed in this work are solely those of the author and do not necessarily reflect the views of the publisher, and the publisher hereby disclaims any responsibility for them.

ISBN: 978-0-595-43442-8 (pbk)
ISBN: 978-0-595-68645-2 (cloth)
ISBN: 978-0-595-87769-0 (ebk)

Printed in the United States of America

PALE IMAGES OF A NOBLER DAY
PEOPLED RELICS HOLD SILENT SWAY
IN DARKENED CORNERS.

STORE THEM AWAY THOUGH THEY ROT
USELESS REMINDERS OF WHAT WE'RE NOT
WASTE PRODUCTS OF OUR HASTE HEAPED HIGH
LOOK NOT BACK, PASS THEM BY

KEEP THEM WHERE THEY BRING NO SHAME
LEST WE REMEMBER FROM WHENCE THEY CAME

ASHES TO ASHES … DUST …
RUST … RUST …

—Laura Lustig 1989

Contents

PREFACE

It has been more than 20 years since I first wrote the pages that follow. Everything written here represents my experiences as accurately as I am able to portray them. Some names have been changed to protect their privacy. While I have made amendments and additions to reflect changes over time, I have kept most of my original thoughts and feelings because they testify to the effects of raising a child like Jesse, and the environmental circumstances that can overtake and diminish an unseasoned parent's sense of self-confidence. Much of the guilt and remorse mentioned in these pages were to be assuaged in later years with the advent of experience, better knowledge and maturity.

Yet, much of what I wrote then still applies. The technological changes that have come along in recent years have certainly improved the services that are offered to children with disabilities and their families. But many parents still suffer tremendous pain in raising their special children, particularly if they are poor or single. Society is still uncomfortable with people whose differences set them apart from the mainstream. And it is still difficult to find comprehensive treatment for all the special needs of many of these children and their families.

This book is for parents. It is for those countless numbers among us who, because of our children's differences, have felt alone, unable to give voice to nameless fears and feelings of guilt, hopes and dreams. It is to help them see they are not alone in their feelings and that we share a common bond. It is also for those less experienced among us who are just starting on the long, emotional tangle of unforeseen pathways, in the hope that from my experiences they will find new insights to light their way.

It is for those parents who have been fortunate enough never to experience the differences I speak of, in the hope that the basic tie beneath our dissimilarities the love we share for our children will bind us in greater understanding and enable us to reach out in new ways.

It is for anyone contemplating becoming a parent, to help them gain empathic insight into the courage and fortitude called for on the part of parents.

This book is also for the professionals in the field and those training to become professionals in the hope that it will provide a useful tool for breaching the gap that frequently exists between themselves and parents of special children.

Lastly, this is a story that must be told, not just because it is my story, but because, in very many ways, it holds parallels for any families whose children do not fit into the mold society sets.

1

A NEW BEGINNING

Our first real home! After moving around from one apartment to another during those first unsettled years, we were finally ready to move out of the cramped quarters in which Lynn and Andrew had been born. It would be a bright, sunny new home in a lovely suburban town where the grass looked greener and the air felt clean and fresh.

Hal and I were young, in love, and full of hopes and plans for the future. There was no mystery to life for us it was ours to make meaningful for ourselves, and to enrich by the new relationships we would create. For we had love and vitality to spare. It was the dawning of the Age of Aquarius for us, a new beginning, the time of our life in the sixties. Hal was making a success of his business venture into the broadcast recording industry.

In our enthusiasm, we pushed aside little conflicts like the old controversy about the isolation of suburban life from the mainstream. We had chosen the relative security of these narrower confines over the broader but less secure side of life in the big city. This security was later to break down as the population shifted from desperate cities to suburban outposts. But never mind. Fate had other trials in store for us, and the relative merits of the question would become merely academic.

For now, we were happy in our move. Having both been born and brought up in the big city, we yearned for bluer skies and greener grass, and a place to find some privacy for our thoughts. We had two beautiful children, a third on the way. Pretty, vivacious, dark-eyed Lynn age four, was everything I wanted in a little girl. Even at her birth she had seemed perfect, without the tiny, wrinkled look usually associated with small babies her size, and with a full head of hair, perky eyes, and full round face.

Andrew age three, was the epitome of what a little boy should be, it seemed to me, with boyish curiosity, a little clumsy perhaps, but delightfully impish. Together they were charming and lovable.

Life seemed made to order, smooth and untroubled. Hal and I lived in the euphoria of egotistic youth. Nothing seemed too much to accomplish and the world was ours. Indeed, in our naiveté, we could even entertain the notion that at least one of our children would grow up to be a benefactor to mankind, perhaps even President.

WORRY SIGNS

He arrived; a handsome baby boy who would develop straight, flowing sandy hair and big green eyes, unlike the rest of the children, with their curly dark hair and dark eyes. We couldn't decide who he looked like, but with such perfect features, such beautiful hair and eyes, it must portend great things in store for us. After all, he will have all the advantages that two highly intelligent and successful parents can give him. As if to confirm our thoughts, the doctors complimented us on our robust, healthy baby boy. We had picked out the name Jesse, and even the name sounded prophetic.

The months passed. The new baby seemed content. He'd been so good, sleeping through the night by the time he was three months old. He'd started on whole milk and solid foods, and one had to laugh at the vigor of his appetite. The other children adored him and were constantly holding him. Some people frown at this, since the children were rather young themselves, but we had confidence in them, and firmly believed that the more handling and physical contact the baby had, the healthier his psychological development would be. In addition, having the other children share in this type of contact, I believed, would help them feel self-assured and enhance their bonding with their sibling. As an educated parent, I had read the baby care books and the child psychology books, and this was considered good practice.

There was to be one moment of fear, but it soon passed. Lynn had been left in Jesse's room while I went down to get a bottle for him. The baby was sleeping and I had put the crib side up for extra protection. Fifteen minutes later, I walked into the room and could not believe what my eyes beheld. There was four-year old Lynn sitting in the rocking chair with the baby still sleeping peacefully ensconced in her lap. The crib side was still up! How did she do it? To have picked up this fifteen pound baby, lifted him over the crib side and placed both of them into the depths of the chair hardly seemed possible for a four year old toddler. At the time, I was in too much shock to even think of questioning her, and I wondered if I had absent-mindedly placed the baby in her lap. Yet, since I was not in the habit of leaving her alone with the baby, it did not make sense that

I would have chosen to take the baby out while he was sleeping. It is a mystery we were never to solve, for years later, talking about it with Lynn, she did not remember the incident. After all, she was accustomed to holding the baby, though in my presence, and this must have seemed like no big deal to her then. Other, less pleasant thoughts will crowd into the mind later, in connection with this incident.

Jesse was growing by leaps and bounds. He seemed a little slow in developing those milestones the other mothers talked about, but why worry, I thought. I was not one of those anxious parents who vacillate between fearfulness and boastfulness about their babies. I felt quite sure Hal and I passed our own good health and strength on to him as we did with the first two children. Life was too full of stimulating and rewarding activities, and I refused to spend time hovering over every move. Besides, I felt I was an old hand at it now, with Lynn and Andrew having given me very few problems. Raising children seemed as easy as apple pie.

There were moments when, tired and more vulnerable, a vague sense of uneasiness overtook me. It all seemed a little too easy. They were so tiny and helpless, the three of them—would they grow up all right? At those times, little dark superstitions from primitive depths sprang up, filling my head with thoughts like: Things are too good; something has to happen to spoil it. What was it I was supposed to do when I had these thoughts, knock on wood?

Then relief would come and reason return. It must be fatigue, that late dinner, or a temporary chemical imbalance. But mind over matter only works so far.

Jesse's physical development seemed far ahead in one respect: he'd already developed a mouth full of teeth. He'd thrown the bottle away at six months, far earlier than Lynn and Andrew, and was practically feeding himself. His appetite seemed enormous, yet he was not getting fat in spite of it.

Something else became obvious. Unlike his left-handed father, he was strongly right-handed. At least we wouldn't have to face that old controversy about left-handed people that Hal had to bear, that is, whether or not to attempt changing dominance before it becomes set. His mother attempted it when he was a toddler, and he had all the frustrations such efforts bring before she finally gave up. For awhile, authorities stopped believing in the attempt to change dominance, but then there was some new research which threw this into question again. With language functions in the left cerebral hemisphere, they said, it is more felicitous to be right handed, since right-handed people have left cerebral dominance, and vice versa. In any event, one could have no doubt about Jesse, since he hardly ever used his left hand for grasping, even to hold the cup. He seemed really lazy about it. Well, I thought, it will come in time.

Only it didn't happen that way. He didn't use that left hand. When lying on his stomach he only seemed to flex his right hand and foot, using them to propel himself over on his back, but his left hand and foot usually were slack. And he was very slow in learning to sit, to walk. He was slowest of all in learning to talk. At one year of age, he was too quiet. My thankfulness at having a peaceful baby was coming back to haunt me now.

Like a good mother, I'd been going to the pediatrician every month, and he asked the usual questions about Jesse's development. My negative responses elicited no comment from him. In general he seemed to say that everything was in order, and this tended to allay any incipient fears. Well, after all, I thought, weren't there lots of famous people whose progress as children seemed inordinately slow but who grew up to be brilliant benefactors of mankind?

The doctor knew that Jesse has been sitting up unaided only a short time. He'd started to crawl, but somewhat clumsily. When asked about language, I explained that he made some consonant sounds, but was saying only two words, mama and cookie. Even these words, however, didn't seem to have any meaningful association.

"He doesn't use mama to call me," I told the doctor, "and if it is a cookie he wants, he merely points or cries until he gets it."

The doctor just nodded.

Now things were becoming less peaceful at home. There were increasing signs of frustration, and temper tantrums were becoming frequent. Hal and I had, from the start, determined that children need firm discipline and such behavior was not to be tolerated. We would not become a slave to these whims of his. This principle seemed to have worked with Lynn and Andrew, but not with Jesse. No attempts to teach him the connection between words and the things he wanted were successful, and no amount of firmness could turn off the tantrums.

At other times, Jesse would show no interest in the bright new toys he was always receiving, but would lie on his back quietly for hours. Something had to be wrong with this fair-haired boy I had selected as the perfection of my dreams. Perhaps it took too long for me to see it, but then, why hadn't the pediatrician said something? Who could be better trained than he to pick up such cues? And I was remembering the rosy picture at the hospital, where they all said such good things about my newborn son. Could this really be my son?

The final straw that would break my complacency for good occurred one day when Hal's mother was at the house, watching Jesse eat.

"Something is wrong with this child," she blurted out. "He's not using his left hand."

Reassuringly, I told her that he's just lazy, but my hands were clenched in a cold sweat.

"Laura, don't argue with me," she said. "I know what I'm talking about. I insist you stop ignoring it and do something."

Now we were staring at each other, a deep look of worry in her eyes, and I was weighing her words. We had never taken her too seriously before. She'd had three miscarriages in her own lifetime, and was always over-protective of her two boys as a result. Her fussy ways drove me crazy with our first two children.

But for once I realized, as I picked up the phone, she was absolutely correct. Time to stop playing the role of the three wise monkeys. Time to remove the hands from the eyes and ears, and speak those words to the doctor that would mean an end to my peace of mind.

I was talking into the phone now, and the questions were coming out in torrents of emotion. This time I was not accepting platitudes.

Finally, he said the dreadful words, in a tone never to be forgotten—as if he were telling me to take two aspirin and stay in bed.

"There is some brain damage," he said, "but otherwise he's a bright little boy. We can take care of him from this office."

The words were unbelievable. Was that me he was talking to about **my** son? Brain damage! Waves of shock and fury shook me. How long had he known! What kind of fool had I been to ignore the obvious and merely accept the doctor's reassuring authority unthinkingly?

Finding my voice again, I asked him to refer me to a specialist. Brusquely, I cut him off as he sought to reassure me once more, demanding a recommendation.

The next phase of my life was about to begin with a round of specialists.

2

BLACK CLOUDS

The neurologist spent a long time examining Jesse, doing things I had never seen doctors do before such as measuring the circumference of his head. What's wrong with his head—it looks perfectly normal to me, I thought. I searched the doctor's face as he worked, looking for some tell-tale sign of what he was finding, but I saw only a matter-of-fact, placid look all the way through. How bad can it be if the doctor shows no alarm, I wondered.

At last the examination was finished. The doctor was facing Hal and me.

The first words out of his mouth brought a rush of tears and my knees went weak. Cerebral palsy! I hardly heard the droning voice as he continued explaining in those sterile, medical phrases, the extent of the damage. He was talking in that 'aspirin' voice while my heart was breaking. A condition I knew only as some dreadful thing that happened to other people had been suddenly brought home to me. Then I heard one hopeful phrase. "The problem is mild," he was saying. "It has affected his left arm and leg, and to a smaller extent, the left side of his face, but he will not be crippled. He will be able to walk and use his left hand as a helping hand."

Exercise and some type of short leg brace, were prescribed. This time I listened to every word of hope desperately. I longed to hear that it's not as bad as it sounded. For once, I would learn, I could trust the doctor's words, at least regarding his physical condition. But this was just the beginning of my problems. The picture was far from complete.

The temper tantrums were getting more intense. It took a while to realize it at first, but Jesse was spending more and more of his day crying. Nights were even worse. He had developed a habit of rocking violently so that his head was coming into contact with the headboard. Moving him down toward the bottom of the crib was useless, for he always managed to move back up. It was as though he was purposely seeking to hurt himself. I listened, across the hall, in my own bed, to the dull thud of his head hitting the crib board, the sound getting louder as the

6

crib inches toward the wall. Hour after hour, night after night, this went on. How could he stand the pain, I wondered. I almost expected to see the top of his head flattening out like a pancake.

Lying there, exhausted physically and emotionally, I watched Hal get up and go to Jesse. His voice floated back, soft, loving words of comfort, cuddling the baby as he spoke. But Jesse continued to whimper unresponsively. Now Hal raised his voice, vainly trying to reach Jesse, if not with love, then with threats. The whimper droned on. Suddenly there was a loud noise followed by hard crying. I raced into the room, to see Hal holding Jesse, patting him, kissing him, soothing him, and looking a little frightened.

"What happened," I asked.

"Nothing," he replied, "Jesse tumbled out of my hands and hit the crib side, but he's all right. Go back to bed."

He shooed me out, and a little while later, as Jesse finally quieted down, came back to bed himself, a drawn and haggard look on his face.

But there is more to this incident than Hal had been willing to tell me, and the truth would only come out much later, when we were both eaten up with guilt and sorrow.

A call to the neurologist the next day did not provide much relief.

"Many so-called normal children develop this bizarre habit," he said. "It will pass."

But how many do it so intensely and for so long into the night? The only answer seemed to be to wear him out with exercise during the day so that he would be too tired to stay up at night. Only I was wearing myself out, too. More and more time was being devoted to Jesse, less and less to the other children. By suppertime, my nerves were frayed and I was impatient with the whole family. This should have been the pleasantest time of the day for Hal. It wasn't.

The worst part of those hours with Jesse was the lack of communication. It wasn't just a language barrier. How do you reach a child who's unresponsive to love, who shows no fear of punishment, who hardly knows you're there except to satisfy his most basic needs for food and physical comfort? It was as though he lived in a different world with an impenetrable shield drawn between us. I found myself looking at this child as though he wasn't human, some strange being in human form but without recognizable patterns of behavior. All my instincts as a mother were thwarted.

"Jesse, let's look at pictures. Ooh, what a pretty picture." (Jesse shows no interest).

"See the pretty flower?" (Jesse looks at his fingers).

"How about this picture. This is a boy, like you. Say boy, Jesse." Silence.

Picking him up, I started to gently jostle him, to tickle him and laugh. Maybe I could shake him up somehow, spark some interest. He started to whine. I brought him over to his toys and showed him how to build blocks, knocking them down with a loud noise. No response. Then his toy workbench, at which I started to bang away, making appropriate noises and trying to demonstrate the principle. The whining increased.

Now I was feeling frustrated and angry, and so I put him into the playpen, leaving his toys around him. He lay there, and the whimper turned into real crying. I picked him up, but the crying continued. What is it, what does he want? Wild imaginings popped into my mind. Maybe this isn't my child. Maybe they switched babies at the hospital. After all, nobody's been able to decide who he looks like in the family. Now I was shouting at him, calling him a bad boy, finally slapping his bottom. Some mother, I thought to myself. I'm doing everything I vowed never to do.

"Stop that crying or I'll put you into your crib for the rest of the day." It was as though he didn't hear or see me.

Then I tried bribing him. "Jesse, want a cookie?" But Jesse didn't take it, and the crying grew worse.

I put him into the crib and ran into another room, my hands clapped to my ears. After what seemed like an eternity, the crying stopped and Jesse went off to sleep just as my nerves shattered.

Such was a typical day, alternating with periods when I simply turned up the stereo and ignored his crying. Only one thing kept me going in spite of the bad times; somehow I sensed that he wanted me to reach him. Tiny little signs that I can't even explain, a look (is it pain?), an occasional smile, even in the frustration he constantly exhibited, I saw a plea for help. Isn't there anyone who could tell me how to help him?

The head-banging receded into the background with the next episode in store for us. Jesse had started hitting himself in the face with his fist, continuously, uncontrollably. He cried only as the bluish bruises began to appear. Panic set in as I tried to restrain him, alternately bribing, distracting, punishing him in a vain attempt to make him stop. Nothing worked. It was as though only the more severe pains reached his nervous system, and only then did he stop, but just until the pain receded. And as I watched, the punches were getting harder, faster, more intense and it seemed with each blow that it was me who was bleeding.

The doctor couldn't tell me what to do here either. He couldn't explain this one away. And out in the street, in public places, there was no way to explain to strangers who shifted their glances at us. Jesse looked like an abused child. I wanted to stop people and swear that I wasn't a child abuser. Instead, I averted my gaze and hurried on.

Gradually, I was to build up a shell toward these people with their hurtful glances. People could never understand, so I closed them out, ignored them. Or else I would stare them down as though I couldn't imagine why they would be looking my way. Acting tough was becoming my face to the world. Even those who didn't look at Jesse, I imagined, were purposely avoiding it because of embarrassment. No one could help but notice this weird child.

How many of those people I must have been unjustifiably castigating. No one could do anything right in my eyes. I started avoiding friends, particularly those who had young children like me. Sometimes we would go out with couple friends in the evening, but I avoided having them know anything but the most superficial side of what I was going through with Jesse. On the rare occasion when a friend visited the house, I could see the embarrassment, the avoidance of asking personal questions about Jesse. Funny how I started off thinking that Jesse lived in a world of his own, and now he was drawing me into that world, too, so that I felt like I was an outcast in society.

Jesse was left at home as much as possible. We were fortunate to have a house-keeper who lived with us. That poor lady spent a lot of her time practically standing on her head to distract Jesse from his destructive behavior. I would take Lynn and Andrew on outings, but not Jesse. And not without guilt feelings, each and every time. Much of the time, however, was spent not only escaping from Jesse, but even from Lynn and Andrew. Yet, while busy with chores or involved in impersonal adult groups that gave me some respite, Jesse's self-inflicted punishment was haunting me. I remembered little things I had read in the psychology books.

What is it the experts of that day would say about Jesse, my battered child? A wish to hurt himself, perhaps? Because his mother was too demanding, had too many ambitions he couldn't live up to? They would have a field day if they only knew what we had planned for him while he was not yet out of the womb. In the literature of the time, mother was always to blame for the child's emotional imbalance. I remember reading that even academic failure for some children could have a psychological cause. The fear of not being able to excel made it easier to fail, so less would be demanded, the experts said. Or it may be the need for attention, even negative attention.

Was Jesse failing to learn normal behavior as a reaction to me? Had I been too stern, too unaccepting? Had those infernal pipe dreams somehow been communicated, as though by osmosis, to him? Or had I been neglecting him, leaving him too much in the care of a housekeeper? Self-destructive tendencies, they would say, because of youyouyouyou....

3

WEDNESDAY'S CHILD

I went to other doctors, visited big hospital centers, therapists, clinicians, psychiatrists. One recommended tranquilizers, but this had a devastating effect on Jesse. The smallest dose sent him into deep depression, followed by a drug-like sleep, and I soon discontinued using them. The only good thing that came from all the visits was the confirmation that Jesse's problems were neurological, not psychological; central nervous system dysfunction, not mother's disgraceful malfunction. But no help for that battering ram of an arm.

The self-torture was growing worse. Jesse would start the moment he woke up in the morning and continuously hit himself, harder and faster, until he screamed with pain. I was spending all of my waking minutes with him, carrying him, holding his arm down, playing with him to distract him. My beautiful little boy was beautiful no longer, with bluish welts around his nose and eyes, and new ones starting in other places when he could not longer take the pain there. What would he do to himself? I was fearful that he would inflict permanent damage.

When no one else could find a remedy, I was to find it at home, through Hal. In what turned out to be a brilliant maneuver, Hal devised a splint out of shirt cardboard rolled up into a cylinder and taped over Jesse's elbow.

I watched the little face so full of misery as Hal approached him and took his right arm.

"Now, my son, let's see if this helps you. Daddy's going to make you feel better, okay?"

The crying stopped as Hal started to adjust the splint. He let go for a moment as more adjustment was needed. Jesse got in one more jab at himself, an angry cry escaping his lips at the same time. Both Hal and I grabbed for him at once. This time I held him until it was finally ready. As the splint went on, Jesse quieted down almost as though he understood from the start what it would do for him. A placid, peaceful look came over his face, and Hal and I stood back, hardly breathing, watching warily to see what would happen. But Jesse didn't even try to reach his face.

He could now raise his hand but not bend it toward his face. Relief was immediately evident and placidity returned to our lives until the worn-out cardboard had to be replaced. The fighting and crying would begin the moment we approached that silly-looking but effective device. Bathing time was a watery battle scene, and I was even spoon-feeding him so we wouldn't have to remove the splint.

How many times a day, now that I could afford the luxury, I stood and looked over at that helpless, sad little boy in his playpen, the bruises looking worse than ever in the healing process, the once-handsome features still swollen out of proportion. How many times did I find myself beating my chest in the intensity of my emotions, as though physical pain would relieve mental anguish. This is laughing fate's answer to a foolish mother's vanity. My way out was found by running away. I spent more and more time away from home, leaving the children in the hands of the housekeeper, a good, kindly lady, but certainly not a replacement for their mother.

I was bringing home lots of clever new toys and games for the children, as if the purchase of these things would take the place of my time. The chemistry set for Andrew, and the plane models ... only he needed someone to do these things with him. The new books and expensive dolls for Lynn ... but who would read them to her or chat with her as she played with the dolls?

I welcomed the stimulation of a variety of activities, political, social, cultural, which kept my mind wholly occupied in other channels (except for the moments of guilt). I was filling my time with community activities, which I could rationalize was productive, except that even when I was home, I was too busy for the children.

With nerves straining, I was frequently sharp when they intruded on my work.

"Mommy, when can we do the airplane model?"

"I don't know, Andrew, not now. We'll do it another time."

"But I want to do it now."

"Stop bothering me and try it yourself. I told you I'm busy now. You can figure out some of the parts yourself."

The airplane model never did get built, and the chemistry set remained unused until the parts got lost as did lots of the doll clothes.

Poor Lynn and Andrew. They weren't responsible for Jesse. Guilt was building up in me like a dam. The response to this feeling wasn't more justice for the children, but less, for one tends to rationalize the need to find escape, bringing more layers of guilt and rationalization, until the vicious cycle entrapped me.

I sought out still more specialists, looking for more answers, but really searching for someone to say, "It's all right, mother, your boy will outgrow it." It is a common phenomenon, this hysterical searching for the right answer. Why do we do it? Perhaps because we are so puzzled by the seeming contradictions in our children's behavior making us despondent one moment and joyful with renewed hope at the next sign of progress. Perhaps it is because we don't want to bear the burden alone, for this means a final reckoning with ourselves. We can rationalize that we are involving ourselves in our children's problems when we are really still running. Whatever the reason, it would appear to be a necessary ritual we must work our way through before wisdom and insight are ours, a physical and mental exercise to the point of exhaustion, before we can rest.

They were using more labels—more dreadful words, things like mental retardation, autistic symptoms, possible institutionalization, and each time it would strike terror in my heart. Each time I refused to accept them. What do these cold, clinical purveyors of doom, with their little bag of tricks, know about my child? They spend a half hour testing him and are ready to close the book on his life's course, on my life's hopes.

"Well, isn't that what you wanted," a little voice says, "someone to tell you what will happen to him?"

But I only wanted to hear good things, for I knew him better than they ever could. I had seen little chinks of light in the darkness. Like the day he picked out a new object in his room too high for him to reach, and he found a way to reach it with a stool, even though no one had shown him how. Finding answers for himself, isn't that supposed to be a sign of native intelligence? And this so soon after he started walking, finally. The joy I felt when he took those first steps. And then the trip to the store to buy his first pair of walking shoes. Almost like a normal mother and baby, that purchase. He was still only two years old, and I'd heard of other children who didn't walk until almost two. He'd also increased his vocabulary, saying a lot more words. They were not meaningful to him yet, but it would come, I felt sure. I even had something to boast about. Jesse had always put his slippers on correctly, right slipper on the right foot and vice versa, which seemed almost precocious at his age, a small but important symbol. There was nothing to go on but a mother's intuition, and I had to laugh as I recalled how once I would have scoffed at other mothers' bragging about such incidentals. Doctors are not God. They don't have all the answers, I reassured myself.

DARK MOMENTS

The last doctor had been seen. Hal had finally put his foot down and said ENOUGH! The moment of reckoning had come, when we had to face up to it, talk it out together and bring into the open everything that had been crammed away in the dark, inner recesses of our minds. We looked at each other numbly at first, with bits and pieces of things learned over three years' time a jumble in our heads.

"What more do you expect to learn," Hal was saying. "Every time you see a new doctor, you find out you know more than they do about Jesse. Or else you won't accept their diagnosis. Maybe they can't tell you what he'll grow up to be like. All they can tell you is what you already know, that he is brain damaged and has severe mental and behavioral problems as a result."

"But there must be some way to teach him," I replied. "Some way to reach him and communicate with him." I felt as though my hands were tied. All the little joyous discoveries children make every day had been denied him, and the pleasure parents take in watching their children unfold like blossoms nurtured with a mother's love, were cut off. Somehow I expected the doctors to tell me what part of the brain was hampering my efforts, what I could do to compensate so that I could get through to Jesse, as though this would make him normal again.

"It may be that Jesse will always have these problems," Hal was saying, and I felt rebellion rising in me at his words. "You're being simplistic, looking for easy explanations to a very complex problem. And anyway, why do you expect anyone to tell you what will happen as Jesse grows up when no one can tell you this about Lynn and Andrew? Who knows what war may someday take Andrew's life, or what troubles may overtake Lynn and cut short her bright promise. All we can do is give them the best we have, and hope they will live full, happy lives."

My tears were coming with his words, bitter, hot floods of self-pity that had been locked up all this time. For the hard truth was that all our searching had been a kind of shadow-boxing. I had been fighting for myself more than for Jesse. What does he know about normality or abnormality? Only I couldn't accept the dashing of **my** hopes, **my** illusions. This smug, private world I had built had isolated me from life. It wasn't a reality, it was a fairy tale with all of us living gloriously ever after, beautiful people creating a beautiful world of our own.

The blow to the ego is worst of all. The knowledge that we have borne an imperfect child has a special effect on parents, and perhaps even more on women. Though our husbands may share this feeling, it is we who carry and nurture the growing fetus in our bodies, and so it seems somehow like a reflection of our incompleteness—blood of our blood, flesh of our flesh, the fruit of our womb that tells the world what we are, or are not. Our children are part of us, and we of them. No matter what our sophisticated intellects say about their individuality as separate people living their own lives, our dreams and emotions are tied up with them in an inseparable bond. We live on through them and in them, even after death. Under all the layers of rational thought and education lies this inescapable, indigenous claim with its first priority on nature.

We may denigrate parents whose lofty ambitions for their children lie brazenly naked for all to see. We may camouflage or mute its truth in the comfort of watching our children's potential unfold. But let this potential be cut short, then in negation it lies exposed, through pain, the raw wound of unrequited nature. Immortality denied.

All the more unbearable, then, if you're a mother who's always been so certain of your capability, a believer that your children are bound to grow up straight and strong because of your smart ideas on good psychology, good nutrition, and good heredity. All the more unbearable in a world that prizes its bright, beautiful children, where all around you are parents proud about their children's accomplishments, and encouraged by an approving society. It is no good to tell us, "Accept your child, love him as he is." We know it, and desperately need to. But we are torn between this and a competing need to make him more like those peers society approves of, to make him more acceptable to the rest of the world. It is easy to ask that we be accepting, but will others? *Wednesday's child has been christened by society.*

In the weeks and months that followed, Hal and I were to question many things we had previously taken for granted or never analyzed. A constant basic theme in our searching had been the need to find a cause for Jesse's problems. No one had ever satisfactorily answered that. Why had it been so important to us? We recognized that even if we could determine the exact etiological explanation for all his behavior manifestations, it would change nothing for Jesse. Unlike physical medicine, knowing the cause does not usually provide a basis for finding the cure. There are no cures. Yet, knowing this, we had never given up looking for answers. Why? Was it that we were looking for something apart from ourselves, outside of ourselves, to blame; something that would relieve us of our burden of guilt? Was there a secret fear of genetics as the cause—a faulty seed? Was it something I had done, through neglect, during my pregnancy?

Thinking back to my pregnancy, I remembered I had gotten sick in my sixth month, and the doctor prescribed some rather strong medicine for fear I might abort. I caused that illness, I thought, with my smug attitude about child-bearing and child-raising. I had kept up all my usual activities, even adding new ones. Like that big, lively party I hosted for so many people, doing all the work myself. It was a week after that when a urinary tract infection hit me hard and I was in bed with a fever that rose as high as 105 degrees. Maybe I should have pampered myself like other women do I thought, or maybe I should have continued my neglect and let nature take its course. And then I would reprimand myself—"Oh, God, what am I thinking".

"Okay," Hal said, "let's have the rest of it. Let it all hang out." And so I told him the terrible thoughts that lay buried deep in the subconscious for so long. The wish that something might happen to Jesse, not of my doing, of course; just an accident, unavoidable. The images that flashed into my mind, unannounced, that I never wanted to admit—a fall down the stairs, a call from the hospital, "Mrs. Lustig, we regret to inform you ..."

And then the shock. *Unnatural mother! Horrible woman!*

Finally the remorse as I looked at this innocent, helpless baby. I loved him. He was still my beautiful child, and he needed me so much. There were still so many little pleasures he gave me, like every time he learned a new word, or made some new discovery. No different than any mother watching her child take his first steps.

Then why do these sinister thoughts invade the mind? Ha! The tables are turned on you, Freud, old man. Children are supposed to harbor a secret death wish toward their parents when their desires have been thwarted, but here's a parent with a death wish toward her own child! How does a mother live with such guilt!

"But you're not alone," Hal was saying. "I have had similar thoughts. We have two other lovely children, with whom we faced only the usual problems until now. Jesse has been a traumatic experience. It is natural," he was saying, "to wish it away as though it had never happened, or will soon end."

The fantasies of our subconscious will not be quieted by moral conscience. Best to recognize it, bring it out into the open, for then I could relegate it to its proper place, a perverse but superficial trick of the mind which cannot dominate two reasonably balanced people. We had been doing everything we could to save the life of our child. And so the confessions tumble out. "Remember the night you heard Jesse fall in the crib?" Hal asked. "I told you he fell out of my arms, but the truth is, I threw him down in anger." Hal had been living with the memory of that sound when Jesse's head came into contact with the crib bars, a sound grown larger and more ugly with memory. Always he had wondered if he caused any brain damage. Now it was my turn to relieve him. "Put it out of your mind," I told him. "Jesse bore no bruises from that incident, nor any symptoms not present before. Whatever damage there was had already been incurred." Yet, though he knew, rationally, that this was so, the scars remained, and the incident could not be remembered without pain.

So, too, my running away from the children blights my memory of their growing years. How many times all three had been left with housekeepers. (Did they ever drop Jesse?) How much I have missed of the moments when I could have been playing with them, reading to them, watching them experiment with their environment and enjoying them; moments that can never be recovered. What they have missed for not having enough of me can only be guessed at. (I was to talk about this with them when they were older).

Ah, no wonder that mothers bubble over with endless talk about their toddler's newest discovery. No wonder, too, that parents are somewhat fearful about having other people, especially little children, hold their baby. Memory carries me back to that moment when little Lynn, left alone in Jesse's room, appeared to have picked him up out of that high-backed crib and brought him over to the rocking chair. But all was well then, reason tells me. Jesse was sleeping peacefully in Lynn's arms. Could I have placed him there absent-mindedly? I was sure I hadn't. Reason would indicate otherwise. I was to go over that moment many times, every detail of leaving the room (I didn't remember Lynn being in the room at the time), the ten or fifteen minutes of being downstairs waiting for the bottle to warm up.

Every incident, not only that one; every possibility of moments when Jesse was left alone, or with someone else, was examined, magnified, in a vain effort to relive my experiences, see something, some clue I may have missed. When was the first time he exhibited behavior traceable to brain damage, I wondered. Was it when he lay in the crib as an infant in that half-flexed position—is that really different enough to be considered a symptom? Or was it later, when the developmental and behavioral symptoms were much more discernible? With so much energy being invested in the search for answers which can pinpoint the moment of trauma, I seemed to be on a repetitive cycle. All my vague fears and guilt had to be concentrated into one area. If it were genetic, I had my role cut out as someone with inferior genes; lucky with the first two, but bound to produce a blemished child as inherent female frailties were tested too far. Hal could not acquire equal share of the blame in this—I reserved the torture, and the pity, all for myself.

Suppose it was something I had caused through physical neglect during pregnancy, or afterward, when Jesse was in the care of nurses and housekeepers. Then I could despise my reckless, neglectful nature and do penance for the rest of my life by giving up everything I wanted for myself in the service of my children. And what of the other children? Would Lynn and Andrew be affected by my taint? Would their children, and their children's children, carry the vulnerable gene?

It all came down to the same thing, though, a need to wreck vengeance on myself for this conspicuous demonstration of unworthiness. And so it went, the self-indulgence and self-flagellation, an outcome of being alone for too long with a problem which became more and more overwhelming.

In later years, with the advent of maturity and professional training, I was able to see how the patterns of my own family upbringing played a hidden role in creating excessive guilt, a need to punish myself. For it is when one parents a child who presents unusual problems or stresses that all the unresolved conflicts from one's own childhood come home to roost. I was later to learn, as I started to work professionally with families having a member with mental disabilities, that feelings of guilt are a frequent companion to the caregiver, and not only when the vulnerable member is a child—I have seen it also when a spouse or elder parent is involved. For many such families, sacrifice and martyrdom become a way of life.

At the time, though, talking about it with Hal was cleansing for both of us. It was like an ingrown infection, blown out of proportion to the original wound, being finally exposed for treatment. We could now reason that no one was to blame. Cerebral palsy is a symptom of brain damage, suffered usually by the fetus either prenatally when illness or mishap to the mother's support system may affect the baby's vulnerable neurological development, or paranatally when the trauma of birth, particularly with prolonged labor, may cause a diminished supply of oxygen.

Jesse had been born through natural childbirth, dismissing any possible dangers from anesthesia, but it was a difficult birth, nevertheless. With two other toddlers to take care of, I had been very active right up to the moment of labor. I can remember feeling weak during the last stage of labor, and almost unable to produce that last spurt of energy called for. The combination of illness and a difficult birth seemed the most logical explanation. There might even be some genetic tendency toward weakened organic functioning during the stress of pregnancy. When Lynn was born, I had contracted a similar infection, which fortunately for her, had occurred after her birth.

I was also able to learn much later that the particular medication, a sulfa pill, prescribed for me during my illness was no longer given to pregnant mothers, possibly because of potential danger to the fetus. One could lay the blame at the doctor's door, but he was using the knowledge available to him at the time, and was alarmed at the hazard to mine and the baby's health posed by the infection and high fever. In any event, no useful purpose could be served for either Jesse or us in this kind of thinking. If I wished, I could find ample reason to see Jesse's condition as genetic or environmental, as my fault or others. He was here, a living, breathing child, with many beautiful ways, deserving of love just for what he is. We are what we are, and can be nobody else.

It was not in my nature to pamper myself during pregnancy, and that has its own merits. Many women do the things I did right up to the moment of birth, with no ill effects. I decided I must not let myself become fearful of life, especially now when my vitality was needed, and I also didn't want Lynn and Andrew to have such fear communicated to them. Life is full of risks we must all take in order to go on growing and learning.

How lucky to have had Hal's strong support to lean on. I don't know if I could have felt this much courage without it. Our bonds had grown deeper with the years, and facing our problems together had drawn us closer. I have learned over the course of years of working with parents that frequently, the experience of having a child with disabilities who cannot live up to their expectations may cause a irreparable rift between the couple. Often it is the mother who takes on all the burdens of raising this child, while the father distances himself from them. I have heard of many instances where marriages have foundered from this kind of strain. In my case, while much of the day-to-day care fell on my shoulders, Hal was always supportive, and frequently involved with me. Mothers (and fathers) often face a difficult decision—whether to give up much of their personal lives in support of their more vulnerable children, or to give up the child for their personal lives. Whatever their decision, it is one they have to live with for the rest of their lives.

The question arises, in such a society as ours where the family unit, even the nuclear family unit, is the cultural, social and economic foundation of our way of life, should people be so alone with choices such as these? The decision to choose one sacrifice over another might not have to be made if there were support services adequate for family needs. (Today, there are certainly more of them than there were when I raised Jesse, but nowhere near enough). We recognize the need for counseling in everyday situations, whether they be personal relationships of married partners or child-related problems. When serious illness visits the family, there are any number of agencies we are invited to call on for help, but when faced with children such as ours, family services in those days were few and frequently too late. There appear to be very few, if any, centers even today, that marshal all the support services needed, medical, psychological, therapeutic and educational, that would enable us to pull our lives together, and plan for our children. And so we run around like chickens without heads, and along the way, lose our sense of balance. There is much compassion due people who must face such burdens as single parents. They have to be even stronger than people like Hal and me. How very lucky we were.

4

A BREATH OF RELIEF

Jesse was getting older, and the gap between him and his peer group was becoming more obvious. Most children at age three have begun to play with or alongside other children, with some form of communication between them. He had needs similar to his peer group, but was isolated from them and alone.

I shuddered at the thought of making any attempt to bring him to other children's homes, for the embarrassment would be more than I could take. I could picture a scene in which Jesse arrives, is greeted and does not answer, is invited to play a game with the other child but does not know how to play cooperatively. He would not talk or communicate in any way with the other child, but would find himself a toy, any little thing he could hold, and go over to some corner by himself. Yet, I knew that what other children learn as though through osmosis, Jesse must be formally taught, if he was to develop mentally. He seemed to feel this too, in his way, for he was a frustrated, unhappy child.

The neurologist was no help here, either, when asked about a nursery school.

"Wait until he's five years old," he said, "and he will be tested for placement in public school."

That's two years away, I thought, and I can't wait until then. Every child needs more mental and physical stimulation than Jesse was getting, and it was too important to be held in abeyance. So I found it myself, a small nursery school in a local Cerebral Palsy Center. He was only there two mornings a week, mostly with children who were severely crippled and couldn't walk or talk. This was hardly what Jesse needed, but at least the teacher would provide some sort of social atmosphere for him. Jesse would also be receiving physical therapy once a week—which was another joke. But it was a start.

I would relish the freedom, too, those mornings, though not without accompanying guilt. I could not seem to begrudge myself the pleasure of having time just for me without a twinge of pain. But what precious hours they were, few though they were; a necessary revitalization for every parent if she is to be a whole person. There was the solace of knowing that Jesse was doing something productive, but also the guilt of feeling that someone else was providing it for him. I felt robbed of that special kind of interaction parents have with their little ones, the sweetness of those innocent years, the excitement of childhood's youthful exuberance. It was a feeling I would never be entirely rid of with each service I sought out for him—that feeling of alleviating my own burden, but also my own involvement. Lynn and Andrew were already in organized school activities at the same time with schedules that kept them occupied after school, either with play dates or other activities of their own choosing. Here, too, that special time just between mother and child was already growing sparse.

Later, there was to be added to Jesse's routine, things like speech therapy, recreational therapy, educational tutoring, etc. It was as though he was a little automaton being put through a series of maintenance to oil and lubricate all the parts that they might work better. An analogy could be found with those so-called normal children who go to nursery school, after which they have their piano lessons, ballet lessons, horseback riding or some other athletic proficiency, and so on up to the moment of bedtime. Today, we are seeing more and more activities crammed into young children's spare time, with an additional focus on academics even before kindergarten. Do such mothers ever have similar feelings of loss of personal involvement, I wonder?

I had started reading everything I could find on the subject of brain damage, and the mountain of literature I came across was awesome. It was ironic that I had learned so little from professionals when there was so much going on in the field. Just knowing that it was such a widespread phenomenon and that many disciplines were intensely involved made me feel less alone. Why did they keep parents in the dark? How much psychological help there could have been in those first moments of trauma and despair. It would appear that here, too, as in so many other areas of medical science, there is a dichotomy between professional and lay people which, either through neglect or design, is largely unbreached. Yet, in that unbreached gap is the child who is the object of concern. Do professionals really expect to achieve maximum potential under such conditions? This was the question that would not stop plaguing me as I became more deeply involved. It was to have long-range consequences for me, leading to a determination to find my own professional niche where I could be of help to other parents facing similar issues.

Through my readings I learned that Jesse's habit of hitting himself in the face was not a form of self-punishment. *Thank God!* It wasn't something psychological and I didn't have to feel guilt over it. Rather, it was the manifestation, of which there are many, of something referred to colloquially as a "tic," or a neurological malfunction that is frequently part of brain damage syndrome. With maturation of the nervous system, and with appropriate behavior controls, many of these disappear in time. As if on cue, the symptom was abating. The splint devised by Hal had been wonderful for Jesse's spirits, and we had become so accustomed to it by now that it no longer seemed like a bizarre contraption to me.

Hal had decided to experiment, over my fearful objections, by shortening the length of the cardboard cylinder, a little at a time, until Jesse could just bend his arm if he tried. He didn't seem to realize what this meant, because he had been unconsciously bending his arm in his movements, yet making no attempt to hit himself. He apparently still needed the crutch, though, since he objected to having it taken off except during bath time, which he was tolerating better, knowing it was temporary, even though it was by now little more than an arm band. Funny kid!

Then came the day I gave Jesse a bath and forgot to put his arm band on. An hour later I remembered and ran to his room, fear clutching my heart that I'd find a bloody face. But there he was, turning a toy over in his hands contentedly; oblivious of the fact that he was not wearing it. I kept that arm band around a few more days, just in case, and then out into the garbage it went, with an accompanying gigantic sense of relief. That night Hal and I had a small celebration in honor of this joyous event.

With the pressure off regarding Jesse's more dramatic mannerisms, I was free to observe attentively other, subtler behavior patterns. That wonderful appetite of his had taken a peculiar turn. I marveled at how much he could put away, without gaining weight. He was rather thin, in fact. His complexion had a pallor to it which was disturbing. He also seemed more susceptible to respiratory ailments than either of the other children, and winters would mean one long, continuous period of colds and congestion.

I wondered, also, about the state of his sensory development. He had a craving for salt, and could eat t alone if allowed to. He loved lemons, and I had watched him eat them in much the same way as other fruit, skin and all, without puckering up at its sour taste. His sense of smell seemed less developed, too. He never seemed to notice odors, not even pungent ones. Then there was his apparent lack of sensitivity to coldness and warmth. He could go outdoors in the coldest weather without a jacket, and also without minding it, seemingly, for I would see no signs of discomfort. He could also be too warmly dressed in hot weather and indicate no awareness. Pain threshold was another matter for conjecture. He had gotten the usual bruises and sores from spills and insect bites without ever crying over them. I knew that other children would have felt them enough to show greater discomfort.

A friend had brought to my attention some experiments being done with autistic children. Though I did not believe Jesse fell into this category, many of his symptoms were similar, particularly these sensory deficits. According to the research findings from the experiments, improvement had been demonstrated in all sensory areas with the addition of something called megavitamins to the diet. This consisted of large doses of Vitamins B, Niacin or Niacinimide (a more easily absorbed form), B Complex, and C. Apparently these vitamins were considered safe in the higher dosages, as opposed to Vitamins A and D, which could be harmful, and they seemed to be in short supply in the bodies of autistic children tested. Theoretically, their bodies could not utilize vitamins as efficiently as normal children, and so much more had to be fed to them. The body then used what it needed, and threw off the rest. Tests had shown very little being thrown off. This could explain why Jesse was so thin and subject to infections, I thought. The vitamin therapy program appealed to me. Since it was at worst, rather harmless in the quantities I would be using, it was worth trying. I had to smile as I remembered the old joke about chicken soup—it can't hurt.

I wrote away for more information, and was impressed with the details that came back. This was a carefully controlled program which had evolved over a long period of intense research and experimentation. A long, multi-level questionnaire form had to be filled out in detail, and our family pediatrician had to be involved as an objective observer. The vitamins then sent to me had to be given in small increments, with notations recorded as to noticeable changes, if any.

Within six weeks after beginning the program, we were sure it had beneficial effects. Our family pediatrician, a kind, patient man to whom we had been referred after the first fiasco, was very much in agreement. Jesse's sense of smell had sharpened to the point where he was obviously sniffing at new, interesting odors, even using it to investigate new foods. The pallor was gone from his face, his odd cravings had completely disappeared and he was eating food in more normal quantities. He'd even started getting finicky, which was all right with me.

Things were definitely on the upswing in other ways, too. The nursery school in the Cerebral Palsy Center must have been a step in the right direction, for Jesse seemed happier, with far fewer temper tantrums. His time there had been increased to three mornings a week. They were working on concept development, which we were reinforcing at home, so that he was finally using words to convey his needs. I brought home stacks of picture books from the library and he would name many of the pictures. Though one-word nouns were still the major part of his vocabulary, he was beginning to repeat phrases. He had quite a facility for mimicking, which was fine as a beginning, since this is the way toddlers begin to learn.

But the mimicry had a negative side too. He was perseverating, which is a form of mimicry in which words or actions are repeated over and over beyond appropriateness. And so I might see him sitting with his picture book on his lap repeating words and phrases unconnected to the appropriate picture.

"Jesse, look at the picture. Say bottle. Say boy." He would repeat my phrases, point and gesticulate like me, but not be looking at the picture to which these words related, and the same words would get repeated over and over.

"Jesse say bottle, say boy" would come back his retort.

This tendency even began to take on a punitive aspect for him as criticism was remembered more than praise, disapproval more than approbation.

"No, Jesse, that's not a cup. Find the cup. No, Jesse, look at me. Do it right." The intensity of my desires was spilling over and affecting Jesse adversely. His most voluminous phrases were in the form of negative verbalizations complete with anger, astonishingly, even though I thought I had been controlling my emotions. What a perverse twist this was, that a child who had previously been unable to respond to our attempts at love, was now picking up even subtle signs of frustration on our part. I knew from the literature that his perseveration was a common symptom of brain injury, and that there were methods to combat it, such as reward for appropriate use, selective inattention for inappropriate usage, etc. In this way, Jesse could learn that appropriate language may be used to control his environment and gain attention to his desires.

Emotional responses were showing great improvement, too. He was becoming more affectionate, responding to us and enjoying the feeling of accomplishment when praised. For the first time, we could all share a sense of communication, opening up possibilities for learning new feelings and emotions. It was just a beginning, but it symbolized a multitude of meanings, for now we could be sure that Jesse had a capacity to feel a larger range of human emotions so long absent that we had wondered if we would ever reach him. But if he had been largely inaccessible to us, he must have been even more so to himself. Thinking of his circumscribed world, one might invoke a vision of being transferred at birth to an alien land in which people had recognizable features, but whose minds could be said to travel on a different wave length. If in such a setting we were unable to decode their language or any means of making contact, and were, from the start, without any basic means of communion upon which to build a secure foundation, would any of us behave differently? We would be tense, fearful, cold, unable to give or receive warmth. Indeed, it is at least theoretically possible that much of the bizarre behavior we see in childhood schizophrenia or infantile autism is in reality an adjustment to a world from which children have been locked out by an unbreachable communication gap.

We know that all human beings have a common heritage of language capacity. The brain, in all its complexity, has many discrete functions, including the encoding and decoding of language, any language. Even more primitive than this is what we refer to as "body language" (the subtleties of which are receiving much attention today with respect to research on sensory-deprived children). Body language is unconsciously picked up by newborn infants and is the first means of communication between mother and child—with or without words. If somewhere in the central nervous system, the processing of language or sensory information is blocked, the result is likely to be a confused, disoriented child. Fortunately for Jesse, he still had much potential capacity intact, but would need a heavily structured environment surrounding him, one in which he could feel the protection of familiarity in his daily routines. From this secure foothold he would be freer to take new steps in the learning process. In such surroundings, many of the multitudinous sensory cues the average child receives almost through osmosis, would have to be formally stimulated.

There is in us, as in other forms of animal life, a kind of invisible antennae in which perceptions are accumulated and stored for further use. In Jesse, the signals were being jammed. He would have to be shown, by experientially arranging situations in which he could learn to understand, not only his own emotions, but the meanings of other people's gestures, facial expressions, tone of voice, etc. A prerequisite for all of his learning, academic and social, would be the establishment of verbal communication, and Jesse was at last well on his way. Now I was determined to take him with me wherever I went: trips to the market, the department store, outings with the other children, anywhere he could acquire experiential stimulation. I would have to talk to him about all the minutiae of details other children acquire with their senses, not taking anything for granted. If we could bridge the gap, feed in information, Jesse would then be able to build on it. Time was of the essence, it seemed to me. These years when most toddlers were accumulating a vast storehouse of information, were precious ones for Jesse, too.

Yet it was hard to ignore, or accept, the embarrassing consequences of Jesse's inappropriate social behavior. There were times I still found myself looking for excuses to leave him at home. Of course, this would bring a wave of remorse. As a reaction, I would take him out and submit to whatever embarrassments fate had in store, feeling like a martyr, perhaps enjoying it. For wasn't it a test of my character? Or was it more like a purge of guilt, and wasn't I secretly enjoying the pain? There was the time in the supermarket. I was telling Jesse about different food products as we shopped, and he got tired. He was always tired after walking short distances due to his heavy brace, a metal and leather contraption strapped to his leg allegedly to maintain muscle tone. So I sat him down at the front of the store and told him to wait there for me. (Thinking about this, I would hesitate today to do the same thing—how far we have come in our fear for the safety of our children). A little later, I went to check on him and found him touching a stranger, who was looking at him as though he were a foreign being from another planet. His habit of touching was inoffensive on its own merits, since he was not approaching any sensitive or inappropriate areas of the body. Whatever the case, I was aware that it is not acceptable social behavior.

As the hot flush crept up my face and neck, I grabbed him, pulling him sharply away. Some teacher! Reflecting back on instances such as this, I realize now that Jesse was attempting, in his own way, to explore the sensation of touch, and perhaps something about the stranger's clothing appealed to him. Or possibly it was his attempt to establish a communication link.

Then there was the time he got lost in the department store and I couldn't find him. He had wandered off when my attention was momentarily distracted. I tried calling him by name, a little embarrassed as customers turned to look at me, but it was of no use. Jesse would not respond to his name even if he were within hearing distance. A small voice whispered, *run away, leave him there,* knowing he couldn't tell anyone his name or address. How do you approach a department store employee and tell them you have lost a four-year old boy who can't speak? I did it, of course, but not without feeling shame course through me, as I explained the situation, and I had to explain rather more than I wished to. Do parents today still feel that kind of embarrassment? Some I have met still do, but mainly because of isolation from the services they need, including help with feelings of guilt or unworthiness.

It was interesting to note the reactions I received from people when I could think about it detachedly. There were those who patronized me with pity, and I wanted to strangle them. Then there were those who looked at me rather coldly, as though there was something wrong with me, not my child. I wondered what went on in their minds. Did they think it was a disease, or that some degeneracy in my nature had produced such a child? Perhaps they thought the child is evil. I have seen people cross the street or pull their children closer to them when passing some more obviously disabled person. What does this convey to their children?

I felt a little more fortunate in that respect. No one could know just from looking at Jesse that there was anything different about him mentally—although, of course, he did limp and wear a foot brace. Many children wore foot correction aids for a number of years, and he was young enough to fit into that category. I found myself hoping he would not grow tall too fast, so he could be taken for a younger child.

It was only when people tried to talk to Jesse that they would notice his differences. Or, if he was sitting in one place for awhile, he would gently rock back and forth. Sometimes he would sit there with a toy in his hands, endlessly turning it over until his perseverative behavior was noticeable to others. He seemed to need to hold something in his hands wherever we went. (Even today!)

When I did get through an outing successfully, I would feel vindicated in what I was trying to do. Jesse was being exposed to people, and he had to learn something from it. Sometimes, I even found people smiling at his antics, as though it was entirely normal for him to behave in that way. Usually, though, they were people far enough removed from the behavior patterns of small children in their everyday lives, so that Jesse's behavior might pass if the contact wasn't prolonged. Huh! Here was another kind of minority group member I was trying to pass. Curious, the feeling I'd get when he came through an event all right, that I'd just pulled the wool over someone's eyes.

Gradually, the pain got duller, and with each new occasion a protective scar tissue grew in the weakened places. My vulnerabilities were well hidden, but the cocoon into which I'd drawn myself only increased the gap of understanding between me and the nearby world. It was a double-edged sword, his public visibility and my shrinking from the cruelty of people who could not understand. Children like Jesse were rarely visible in neighborhoods in those days, and people could not be expected to understand that which they do not see.

I had learned one lesson though. In the weeks that followed the department store incident, I concentrated intensely on having Jesse respond to his name. The peculiar thing about it was, he knew his name—and at the same time didn't know it. He would say things like, "Jesse wants cookie," but could not answer the question, "What's your name?" I had to teach him the connection between the two and we practiced having him come to me whenever I called him from another room, rewarding him with a treat. I also taught him to repeat his address in response to the appropriate question, although the words were meaningless at the time. (There were to be vast changes in Jesse's ability to respond, not only by rote, but in his intuitive understanding about emergencies, in the years to come).

In my eagerness to provide a variety of sensory experiences for Jesse, I did some foolish things too. One of the more gross examples of misjudgment was the evening I took the three children to Lynn's piano recital. Jesse enjoyed music, I reasoned, and I wanted to expose him to the sound and vibration of live music. But the concert was long and the room was stuffy at the piano teacher's home. Poor Lynn, pretty, talented Lynn, whose forgiveness I must beg for my insensitivity to her feelings, and Andrew's too. How often I thought about the moment in the middle of her performance when Jesse started making a moaning sound, which grew louder, then he began darting all over the room, looking for toys, talking out loud as I tried to control him, and finally rushing out of that small, crowded room full of people, feeling their stares burning through me. I had to be more careful of the other children's feelings, I thought. Mustn't let them bear my burdens.

5

BABY STEPS

This puzzle is a child unclassified,
We can't place him with children all stratified.
So come let us see if the pieces adhere.
Please have a seat, mother ... over there.

Now, gentlemen, it is my impression,
That this child is lacking in sensory perception.
With hyperkinesis and nervous system etiology,
He surely could use the help of neurology.

I am sure you are right, but from my perspective,
This child's reactions are clearly dissociative.
His problems derive from infantile psychosis.
For which the best perspective is through psychiatric diagnosis.

As I see it he demonstrates signs of being alexic
Perhaps it's because he's somewhat dyslexic.
His visual discrimination seems low,
And by the way, his auding responses are slow.
We'll refer him for tests by the audiologist,
And don't forget about the speech pathologist.

Have you heard of the new treatment they call optometrics?
For the rest we'll rely on the usual psychometrics,
In which his Bender Gestalt shows emotional lability,
And Binet is not significant for language disability.

In bilateral coordination he's poor,
And tactile dexterity is unsure.
So which do you think he needs more,
The physical or occupational therapy floor?

To conclude this study, my fine colleagues and staff,
Perhaps we should call for an electro-encephalograph.
All right, mother, come see what we have done.
You may pick up the pieces, don't drop them, any one.

Jesse was outgrowing the nursery school. He was not yet of age for placement in public school, for the state's responsibility started at age five. But he was in need of a more structured and stimulating environment.

The contrast between his environment and that of the other two children was vast. Lynn and Andrew had been in nursery school since they were three years of age, five days a week, experiencing a varied, richly stimulating program, and Jesse, who needed this the most, was receiving little more than the barest minimum.

I had worked as a trustee with the Director of the nursery school where happy little children came to play, experiment, and laugh with their playmates. Watching them in their bubbling, active world, I wished there was some way Jesse could be taken into their midst.

"And when is your youngest child going to be ready for us," the Director was saying innocently, an inviting smile on her face.

Her words brought a flush to my face. I thought of all the times we had sat together, the Director and the parents of the school, talking about our children, watching parent-effectiveness films, and expressing with outspoken honesty our thoughts and concerns about our normal youngsters. But I had never brought up Jesse, beyond stating perfunctorily that I had a younger third child. Now I couldn't find the words to answer her question. This woman with whom I had worked so closely over the past two years, with whom I had shared so many intimate thoughts concerning children, suddenly seemed like a stranger. She was waiting for my answer.

"Jesse is brain-damaged," I finally blurted out. "He can't function on the same level as these children."

"I'm sorry to hear that," she said, "but why don't you bring him over and let me see him. We've had children with learning disabilities among our population. Perhaps we can find a place for him here."

Oh, yes, yes, yes—could you, would you? "That's very kind of you," I found myself saying, "but I don't think Jesse would fit into the group. Thank you, anyway."

"Will you bring him over to see me and let me be the judge?"

"Of course." But I knew I never would.

Jesse was also outgrowing his leg brace, although here too, the Cerebral Palsy Center had not given me much direction. It had proven helpful for the first two years, stretching the muscles so that he could walk more appropriately, but since then there had been no noticeable difference. On the contrary, it seemed to be handicapping him more because of the added weight on his foot. He dragged it heavily and tired quickly on walks.

I remember the scene at the Cerebral Palsy Center when Jesse came up for review at their clinic. There was a long table, with many people sitting at it, facing us; the orthopedic surgeon looked for all the world as though he is holding court, with the psychologist, social worker, therapists, secretaries and administrators feeding him papers or responding to his smallest gesture. I sat among a crowd of diverse people, young children in wheel chairs, old people, working men requiring rehabilitation, all waiting to be called. I felt small and insignificant, and I knew then what a welfare client must feel.

They shuffled their papers, talked in low monotones among themselves. Finally, my name was called and I noticed, as I brought Jesse up to them, that they never looked at me or acknowledged my presence in any way. They all stared at Jesse, like some piece of merchandise laid before them. Then they began to talk to each other again, referring to statements in their papers.

"Okay, let's have the child undressed down to his underpants."

I looked around for some area of privacy, but they were obviously waiting for me to get on with it and be quick about it. I helped Jesse undress, feeling a loss of dignity about the whole public scene, yet helpless to address it.

"Walk to us, Jesse. Good. Now walk to mommy." Then finally looking at me, a few questions about his progress at home.

"Well, we'll change the leg brace for a larger size and see him again in six months. Thank you, Mrs. Lustig, you can get him dressed again."

"But how long will he need the brace, doctor," I asked. "It seems too heavy for him."

"That's all right, he will get stronger. The brace should remain on until the bone structure is fully developed. We will probably want to remove the brace when he reaches his teens and see how he does without it."

"Will he walk more normally as a result of the brace," I asked.

"He will probably never walk normally. Usually children like him require a bone fusion to give them better use of the leg."

"You mean a leg operation?"

"That's right, Mrs. Lustig" (impatiently). "Now we really must see our next patient."

My mind was in a state of confusion. What was the brace doing for him if he would need an operation anyway? The thought of having to operate on his leg was upsetting too, especially since he was walking well enough to participate in some sports and games. Even the operation, they were saying, would not significantly improve his gait!

So, on my own intuition, I removed the brace one day, but continued the exercises for his left arm and foot which I had been doing since he was two years old. The improvement was immediately obvious as his walk became more springy, and his stamina increased. Yet, even here, countermanding the recommendations of authority figures left me ill at ease. I wondered if I could be causing Jesse irreparable harm in muscle tone and growth. I still could not think of professional advice in terms of relative merits, the advantages versus the disadvantages of a course of action for Jesse personally. Either they were right, in which case I was guilty of arrogant neglect, or they were wrong. Years later, I would learn of the controversy in medical circles regarding the use or disuse of braces for children like Jesse. In other words, there are no absolutes amongst the experts either. Jesse, however, was to develop unusually good flexibility in his affected limbs, thus laying the matter to rest. I never did have the operation for him.

NEW HOPE

In my travels, I had often passed a small, private school, about which I knew nothing. Having no idea where to send Jesse next, and with some curiosity about the nature of this school, I stopped in and inquired. To my utter amazement and delight, I was told that the school was geared for children with physical and mental disabilities, accepting children age three to sixteen. With hardly concealed excitement, I talked to them about Jesse, and an interview was arranged.

As I drove home, my whole mind was working on that interview. I must get Jesse ready for it so that he will put on the best appearance possible, I thought. Rehearse him again on his name and address. Make him look me straight in the eyes as he talks to me, not down at his shoes the way he usually did.

"Answer the nice lady when she shows you pictures, Jesse, and no rocking."

I had given very little thought to the school itself. A perfunctory question or two of the director, in which I practically fed her the answers I wanted in my need to see this as a good placement.

"Oh, yes, Mrs. Lustig, you are so right. Our goal is to bring these children back into the mainstream so they may be placed in public school as soon as possible, for we have many on our waiting lists."

The official-looking literature and application blank seemed reassuring that it was a qualified school. Also, the Director didn't seem terribly anxious to find new students.

"We won't be able to tell you whether Jesse has been accepted until the interview report is brought before our Board of Trustees," she said. "We only accept students whose potential is greater than their present functioning. If he is accepted, he will be placed on the waiting list for the first available opening."

The interview went better than I expected. Jesse was alert and he answered the simple questions put to him. My tensions were relieved by the shortness of the interview, and I was delighted when the Director complimented me on my fine, intelligent son. There was one obstacle, however. All children had to be toilet trained. Jesse wasn't, but I had the summer to work on it. I wasn't going to let that get in my way. I was bubbling over with happiness at my good fortune as I told Hal about the new school. "The Board has accepted Jesse," I told him, "even though there is a waiting list. They must have seen something special about him—they seem to have placed a priority on him as a student."

Jesse would have a real school to go to at last. He could spend a five-hour day there, five days a week. There would be a speech therapist, an occupational therapist, trained teachers, everything he needed. Of course, careful, practical Hal asked a lot of questions about the school I couldn't answer, but I reassured him I would do some investigating over the summer.

Now it was time to really get to work on Jesse. He'd been lazy for too long, I decided, and I hadn't really disciplined myself to the task of toilet training. So it became a day and night intensive training course. To hell with Dr. Spock's warnings and Dr. Freud's personality types. This was more important.

As the summer drew to a close, I was feeling confident. Never mind that I was scolding a lot and driving both him and myself crazy with our ritual every few hours of going to the toilet. So what if Hal came home to hear me alternately coaxing and scolding while Jesse sat on the toilet, until he would finally send me away and offer to take over. We went up to the line, and finally, two weeks before the new term was to start, Jesse caught on. I felt the triumph of success at having gotten Jesse through this with flying colors. After all was said and done, he didn't seem too upset about it, either. I praised him as though he had just graduated with honors.

Those questions Hal had asked still had no answers. The school had been closed all summer and I had no way of reaching the Director. Well, I thought, it could wait for September. I could hardly wait, myself, I was so excited. Everything was going so well lately. It must be a good omen for the future.

The letter announcing the first day of school came in the mail, and my cup runneth over. I was laughing and singing again like I used to when I was young, so long ago. So long ago? But Jesse was only three-and-a-half.

The first day of school for Jesse arrived. I packed him a good lunch in his bright new lunchbox, and he looked spanking clean and shiny in the new school clothes. He would be the best dressed boy in school, I thought. I had finally found out that the school was licensed by the state, and all the teachers fully certified. The quarters in which the school was housed left something to be desired, being an old building which had once served commercial purposes. I wondered about the gym, with its hard cement floor, and some of the rooms seemed a bit small. However, if the state had approved the school, I reasoned, who was I to find fault with it.

I'd met some of the parents, and they seemed pleased with the program. Transportation was our responsibility, and the out-of-the-way carpool I arranged with the only other parent in my area lengthened considerably the trip to and from the school, but it was better than nothing.

The first day kept me at home, close to the phone, just in case anything went wrong. But nothing did. How really clever to have found the school on my own, I thought. Everything I had done to this point had been on my own initiative, and I was feeling pleased with myself.

With all three children in school, I suddenly realized I was able to go back to a normal existence again, doing what all those other nice, normal suburban mothers were doing: decorating my home, attending theater matinees, chatting at coffee klatches. For the first time, I was becoming better acquainted with people in the neighborhood, and thoroughly enjoying a routine, even humdrum, life.

Please, no more excitement, I thought. Just let me have time for myself. Yet, I was strangely uncomfortable in my new role. I couldn't talk much about Jesse with the other mothers; it was too difficult. The discussion would be directed toward Lynn and Andrew whenever I was questioned about my children. The most I would say about Jesse was that he had some learning problems and got special tutoring. The less said, the better, I thought. But try as I might, somehow it was hard to feel like one of them. Underneath the pleasantries, there was still the feeling of being alone, different. I don't know whether I imagined it, or whether my experiences had truly set me apart. I only know I desperately wanted to be like the other mothers.

My peaceful existence was not to be long-lived, however. For soon the parents of the school were calling an important meeting, which I was urged to attend. The internal problems of the school were about to invade my privacy. This was to be the beginning of a long involvement in the complexities of private schools, state laws, educational needs, and the whole spectrum of the political bureaucracy that affected our children's school career. For better or worse, it marked a turning point in my life, the end of an era.

6

LEARNING CURVE

There is a special fondness in my heart for the group of parents I met at Jesse's school. They were a new experience, one which was to prove fruitful in opening up rewarding experiences for me. Through them I would be brought out of my shell, and learn to feel compassion for others whose problems were no less, and in some cases far greater than mine. I was to maintain a close relationship with many of them over the next five or six years, brought together as we were by common needs, pursuing common goals. At last, I had found people with whom I could talk, frankly and openly, about my child and theirs, and they were a source of comfort. With them I would also feel the special vulnerability of parents like us, making normally intelligent, sophisticated people an unwitting prey to our fears and others' ambitions.

I met the parent group of the school early in the year at a social function that was held to welcome everyone back. We heard a pep talk and lots of good hopes verbalized for the new year. It was a good feeling to be among a group of people who were actively involved in their children's education.

Now the meeting I attended had a different purpose. The school was in trouble. The Director was talking about state education officials wanting to close the school, how unreasonable they were being in their demands, how she had a constant uphill battle with them because she put the children's interests ahead of conformity to theirs. Why would the state's interests be inimical to those of the children, I wondered.

The Director talked about specific demands. She had been given three weeks to have a new floor put down in the gym, walls painted, repair work done, and fire safety devices installed. Three weeks, or the school would be closed. There was no money to hire people; that meant the children's fathers must spend the next three weekends doing grueling work. One after another, the men stepped forward to volunteer, Hal included.

Next item: there wasn't enough money to last the year, we were told. The state, which by law paid the tuition of all those students five years of age or over (parents of children under five paid privately), had legislated too little money to provide for professional and ancillary staff, adequate materials, and rent. The parents would have to form a fund-raising committee. The amount to be raised sounded formidable. I volunteered for the committee, but there was that old feeling of fear and anxiety in my heart again. Looking around at the faces of the others, my fear was mirrored in their eyes. Nobody thought to put questions to the Director, least of all me, such as: why have the conditions in the school been allowed to deteriorate without doing something about them? How long had the state education department been warning her of these conditions before they gave her the three-week ultimatum? Why isn't there enough money to carry the school when the tuition rate is higher for special education than for regular education? And why had they waited until now to appraise their financial condition when they had an accountant working for them, a lawyer on their advisory board, and parents in all walks of life who might have provided additional help? How had the school been managing these last three years of its existence? All these questions, and more, would later seep into my numbed mind, but not now, not in this moment of new urgency.

Interesting thing about living in a state of emergency—one becomes accustomed to it after awhile. The mind and body are at a constant pitch of excitement; as the adrenaline flows, you feel more alert, more active. One might even think I was beginning to enjoy it. Like living on a constant high. There seemed to be a certain level of activity my body had learned to require, so that back there at the beginning of the term, when I had the choice of a respite, I was soon hopping around again. I told myself it was a good escape from personal problems, but my choice of activities was pretty exhausting. Rushing around in the car, working long hours in the night has to mean something more. It's almost as if I couldn't come down from this driving need to keep going, keep the adrenaline pumping.

I also didn't have anything like the patience or calmness that once characterized me. Remembering when Lynn was a toddler, all the hours I spent reading to her, teaching her, talking to her. And then with Andrew, even though there were two babies dividing my attention, I still felt pretty cool. So cool, in fact, that I decided to have another child rather soon afterwards. Raising children seemed easy. Now, any little ruffling of the feathers made me over-react. It didn't seem to take much to send me off into a frenzy, doing the thing I swore I would never do, yell at the kids. Then I'd feel terribly remorseful, yet I couldn't show it to them.

They must not see my weakness, take advantage of it. Besides, what do the books say about the importance of consistent treatment? That's it, consistently bad.

Hal did his back-breaking work over the next several weeks, and I dropped everything else to work on fund-raising. Somehow, that year, in spite of more emergencies that kept raising their ugly heads, we got through it. Jesse had some fine, dedicated teachers, and he learned a lot in that one year. He was now recognizing all the basic colors by name, could count to ten, and could place pegs in the correct geometric shapes on a board. He was becoming more independent at home, too, dressing himself except where he needed help because of his weak left hand.

The teachers seemed very hopeful about him. This hopefulness was to remain a characteristic of every relationship Jesse would have with educators who got to know him well. They would always come to recognize more innate qualities than were at first apparent.

Jesse's language was improving, too. He was not only using words meaningfully, but had acquired the ability to speak in short sentences, at least enough to make his needs and desires known. He could also follow simple commands. As the end of the year approached, the Director had begun to sound euphoric again. More pep talks about next year, then the announcement of a summer school program for the children, something I wanted very badly. An assistant director was being hired to run the summer school, as the Director was off for a badly needed vacation, she told us. As a matter of fact, that was the last we would ever see of her, or of her school.

The assistant director did run some sort of summer school program that year, if it could be called that. The outdoor yard of the school was concrete and rather small. Inside there was no air conditioning and the rooms were small and hot. There was no money for materials, so parents donated whatever they could. The program consisted of little more than a baby-sitting service. By now most of the parents were suspicious and worried about next year for the children. A few of us who sat on a showcase board of trustees did some private investigating with the help of the school accountant and the new assistant director, who seemed genuinely concerned and they made some interesting discoveries.

The Director, it turned out, had been taking an inflated salary, with calculated raises every year. Additional monies had been used to supply services at her home. Very little money had been spent in purchasing equipment. To her credit, it must be said that she was not miserly in her hiring practices and had selected a generally good staff. But there would be no funds with which to open the school in September. Nothing was left of the fund-raising efforts supplied by the parents, and since tuition from the state was always late in coming through, there would be no way to pay for salaries, rent or supplies over the first three months; in short, the school could not open in September.

We learned a few general facts about private schools, too. There were many such private schools in the state, and probably in many other parts of the country as well, run on a non-profit basis in order to fulfill state tuition requirements. Non-profit does not mean money well-spent or well-regulated by any agency. It does mean that money must be spent on services and cannot be taken out of the school as clear profit. But with no guidelines on what constitutes an appropriate salary, or what constitutes a valid educational program, the gap is filled according to the judgment of private administrators. It must be said that this is a thorny problem, for with more supervision by the state comes more controls of a bureaucratic nature, diminishing the degree of flexibility, initiative and dynamic interaction that is so important for our special children. That there were, and are, many excellent private schools which not only fulfill their moral and ethical requirements, but are adding to our fund of knowledge new ideas for working with our more challenging populations, has been proven many times over. That there are no hard and fast answers to what constitutes a valid educational program for so many diverse kinds of children, hardly needs to be said. But that there were very few protections from less desirable business operations, existing mainly for a profit motive, needs also to be considered; there were many of these schools opening up as the list of customers grew.

Schools of the more shady nature owed their existence to the fact that there were frequently too few public school classes to house all children with disabilities capable of learning in a classroom situation. At a time in our history when we were finding ever more labels to describe distinct learning disorders, we were ironically facing an ever greater squeeze on state budgets for education. Thus, the public school classes that did exist were geared more for the minimal type of disorders, with good prospects of eventually phasing such children into a normalized curriculum. For many others, the large state hospitals or so-called state schools became the repository of wasted lives. Those parents who could afford it, might pay for residential schools. For the rest, the private schools helped close the gap to fulfill state requirements.

OPENING THE NEW SCHOOL

It was a huddled group of parents who sat with the assistant director talking over the situation. There was one month left of summer, and no prospects for the children in the fall. Though they were of varied ages and abilities, these children had been sent here by each of their school districts because there were no public school classes adequate for their needs. The alternatives for the children were very slim. It would take the school districts months to find new placement, if any at all could be found, during which time there would be only one or two hours of home tutoring provided. Those private schools which were providing a good education were either filled to capacity or too far away for the children to travel back and forth each day.

It had been a good year for Jesse in spite of all the emergencies. He had made progress and he felt the delight of accomplishment. It was showing in his personality development, and I knew how important it was for him to feel some confidence in himself. He was by now a rather pleasant child, and the whole family loved him. He showed high motivation to do those tasks he could accomplish, but he would lapse into a dream-like state at other times. There was still no initiative on his part to play appropriately with toys or games as other children his age do. Instead, he would sit placidly in a corner, frequently rocking, until directed to do something, and even then I had to do it with him.

The prospect of having him at home with very little to do all day was too awful to contemplate, as it must have been for the other parents, too. Yet, he was approaching the age when the school district must provide education for him. The laws of the state required placement for every child who reached five years of age and was capable of learning. There was no requirement, however, regarding the number of hours of schooling, and so, if nothing else turned up, my district would have to put him on the bare-boned minimum of home instruction, which, as far as I was concerned, was no alternative at all.

"Could the parents open up a school, and would the assistant director, who had been so helpful and sympathetic in our plight, take on the role of Director of the new school?" We put this question to him.

"There is no reason why parents could not operate a school," he replied, "and act in much the same way as a board of trustees does in other institutions. The parents could thus be the business administrators, hiring the Director, whose job would be the educational administration of the school."

"Do you have the professional and experiential qualifications?"

"Yes, I do."

"Could it be done in one month's time?"

He would take care of the paperwork and protocol, if the parents would locate new quarters. Two of us undertook this job. One month to find new quarters, receive state certification, acquire staff, notify school districts that the school is qualified for the placement of children with mental and physical disabilities, and have everything in order for the first day of the term. It seemed an impossible task.

Thinking about it later, we had extraordinary good luck. A church building was found, located near a large park, with Sunday school facilities that could be used on weekdays. How wonderful a change from what we had known. No more worries about meeting the state building code since it was already a qualified, operational school for the congregation's children, and it had a park instead of a small cement square between buildings. We were very grateful to the church fathers, to whom we would contribute the costs of our expenses for the use of the building.

The new Director asked some of the last year's teachers to form the nucleus of a staff for the school. Only a few accepted, however, and who could blame them? They'd been burnt once. They didn't even know if the new school would remain operational, but then, neither did we. Somehow, the doors opened on time. Only a handful of the original school population remained, but all districts had been notified, and the state had given us provisional certification.

The parents who would make up the new Board of Trustees each had to sign a personal note for a bank loan in order to operate the school financially for the first few months. A great risk, indeed, since each of us was now personally liable for any deficit; a risk, however, that each parent gladly undertook. We were all excited and confident about our venture. For now, we felt certain, there would always be a place for our children as long as it was needed. No child would be turned away if we could help it. Here at last was safety, for with the administration of the school firmly in the hands of the parents, whose major interest in having a good, viable education for their youngsters was foremost in their minds, it had to be an improvement over the financially and ethically bankrupt morass we had just left.

Poor babes in the woods. Successful and experienced though we all were in our own businesses and professions, and in spite of all the accumulated intelligence and good will of knowledgeable parents, we were about to step from the frying pan into the fire. The next two years would bring to a painful climax the agonies of all the years before, and both Hal and I would come close to losing our health over the strain.

7

A CRISIS IN THE MAKING

There are in the field of special education, many dedicated and highly competent people. They are to be found amongst teachers, administrators, therapists and related ancillary service providers. Many of these people have become involved because of personal contact with someone who has a mental or physical disability, arousing a new sense of awareness. Some may even themselves have had frustrating experiences as children because of a minimal brain dysfunction, which in all likelihood, was not diagnosed at the time. This kind of involvement may arouse a strong sense of purpose and a keen understanding of these children. In the knowledge that one's strengths can be used to salvage a life lies the development of our finest humanitarian instincts; there is no more satisfying achievement than this, and the benefits are both personal and general. True advancement of a civilization is not to be observed merely in the recounting of new technologies, but the extent to which the lives of people, even the least among us, are made more meaningful; that is the measure of a society.

This ideal is universal. Those of us who seek purpose in our lives look for ways we can leave something of ourselves, some small contribution to the building of a culture, whether through our family, community, or beyond. If war tears down, we are unable to accept the stark reality of its destructiveness without here, too, finding a rationalization in the more acceptable ideal. And so armies are always sent to fight a less moral enemy, one we are told, who threatens us or must be made to see our better way of life.

Whatever the reason for entering the field, there is no doubt that the large majority of special educators give a sizeable chunk of themselves to the work if they are to be effective. They must work harder, endure more frustration, and have more devotion to long-term goals than is generally true of others in regular education, in order to be successful. This is not to deprecate the role of the educator in other branches, all of which have their own special problems and frustrations. But progress for children with mental challenges is slower, more painful, more difficult to achieve and requires more patience and special skills to bring about than is required for the average child. Such children don't learn in spite of the teacher, which other parents may have the comfort of feeling as a last resort; to the extent they learn at all, it is *because* of the teacher.

Why do they go on with it, these gluttons for punishment? It could be said they do it for money, since it is generally acknowledged to be more lucrative than regular public school education. But these teachers generally put in more hours, both in college preparation and in sheer work which is mentally, physically and emotionally exhausting. Anyone willing to expend that kind of energy in other branches is very likely to receive similar remuneration. The feeling the teacher gets however, when she has reached a child whom the world has given up for lost, seen him take that small step of progress, is beyond description. She knows it is because of her, nobody else but her. That is the carrot which makes her go on fighting for a child.

There is a quality about the child himself that is very endearing; the trust, so freely given, the eagerness to please, the simple innocence that wraps itself around the teacher's heart and holds her in its grip. She gets to know the whole child in a way the average teacher never does, for she will work longer and more intensely with every aspect of his development in the attempt to provide the most favorable environment for growth. The investment in time, energy and emotions can be consuming. One has to be careful, for it is all too easy for such a child to wrap her around his little finger. She wants to protect him, but she must expose him; she wants to do much for him, but he must be made to do for himself.

Such a teacher faces the danger of losing objectivity; impartiality is out of the question. She no longer sees the child in comparison with his normal peer group—each small advance is a victory in itself. She has her moments of despair, but mostly she is full of optimism in her daily work, an optimism generated by the child himself. It is the sunshine of his world to see his enormous efforts (he has to work so much harder than the average child) greeted by a warm smile; his motivation as a result is that much greater, communicating itself to her.

Jesse was fortunate to know teachers like this, both male and female, and we are eternally grateful to them for their love and humanity. The progress he has made, which is considerable, owes no small measure of debt to their prodigious efforts on his behalf.

How unfortunate then, that the good work of such dedicated people must be offset and counterbalanced by the work of another type of person, also attracted to the field. Such a person is a danger to himself, to the children, and to the parents whose lives are affected by him. The disturbed mind of such individuals may be seen in childhood. They go by different labels, when they are diagnosed, which is usually in childhood, if at all. Direct observation is more difficult in adulthood, for by then they have learned the art of camouflage; their cleverness and social adroitness enables them to blend into the mainstream of society. Only those whose misfortune it is to cross their pathways can come to see this hidden side of their nature, and only when they have overstepped the bounds of propriety so acutely as to come to the notice of authorities can they then be observed and identified. Disturbed personalities, they see the world through a warped mind.

While found in all walks of life, such people are particularly attracted to children or adults with whom they may sympathize, but who also represent the more guileless, vulnerable members of society. Their need is to control, to hold power over others. Along the way, their veniality may become exposed, for the more power they get, the more corrupt they may become. Psychologists refer to them as sociopaths, a phenomenon identified only in more recent years. Nobody who works closely with such a person can avoid being mentally battered. He will stir up conflict; he will lie and steal if necessary, to accomplish his ends. He feels no moral conscience for any wrongdoing, and in fact is not even aware of his wrongs. Frequently he will distort meanings and vilify the character of those he regards as his enemies. His opponents are many and his friends are few, for there are no trustworthy people in his eyes. He may fly into a rage at the smallest sign of frustration, at which time his basic irrational nature may be seen. But this is soon covered up with more lies as rationalization for his actions, and blame is shifted to others around him.

Insofar as their illness permits, such people may function at a high level of ability. No effort is sustained for very long, however, without their unstable emotions getting in the way. They may be knowledgeable about their field and verbally proficient, so as to sound convincing to those colleagues who deal only peripherally with them. In this way, they may gain a stranglehold in a position of power, and woe to those who will find themselves at their mercy.

I was to speak with many professionals in the field of mental health at a later point, when the experiences I am about to relate were behind me, and found a remarkable unanimity in their description of sociopathic personalities they had encountered with similar behavior patterns.

Such a person, we were to find, had gained control of our children's lives, and of us.

INNOCENTS UNDER FIRE

Troubles at the school were all external at first. Teachers' applications for certification had been filed with the county; papers had to be approved for school operation. Somehow, these were slow in forthcoming. Documents were being lost at county offices; officials couldn't be reached after numerous phone calls. It appeared as though, whether intentional or not, impediments were constantly obstructing the school's operation. School districts, as a result, were reluctant to send children until official approval was received. The Director and a determined group of fathers, however, were soon to rectify this. Lawyers, educators and those with business acumen amongst the group were put to work. County and state officials were hounded until the necessary papers were forthcoming. In the meantime, loans were floated to support school services, and contracts and by-laws drafted.

Slowly at first, placement at the school was being sought by nearby school districts for their needy children. The rate of application was to increase, and districts seeking placement would become more widespread within the next two years. At the end of the first year, we would have twenty children; by the second year, this number would more than double. The intent of our group of founders was to make of this small, private school a model of propriety and good education. Every governing law would be followed faithfully, but more than that, all monies would be spent in accordance with sound educational principles. The books and records of the school would be open for scrutiny by any public official and the guidance of financial experts would be sought.

It was believed that the parents, operating as a governing Board of Trustees, with the ability to hire or fire the educational director and oversee all financial operations, would be in the best position to keep the school purposes pure. Provision was made in the by-laws for incoming parents to be elected to the Board, thus building-in an orderly, democratic transfer of power and freshness of thought. All this had been discussed and agreed to by the Director in the initial meetings.

One small distress signal had been telegraphed to the parents at these early meetings, had they been willing to recognize it. The Director had been asked for a reference from his last place of employment, but he had taken considerable insult at this request. After all his time and efforts spent on behalf of the parents' interest, did they still require proof of his good character, he wanted to know? Of course not, the parents told him. Yet, which of us would hire an employee with responsibilities of such magnitude on this basis in his own business? Not one. But then, in a strictly business situation, our vulnerabilities over a helpless child would not have been involved. Only later would this error of judgment come back to haunt us. Later we would discover that under no circumstances would a good reference be obtainable. Indeed, he had been fired for cause in his last position!

The authority of the Board was defied very early in the game. A reasonable budget had been agreed upon, within the confines of tuition payments from the districts, providing also for moderate payments on loans as enrollment increased. But with the enrollment still small, teachers and aides were being hired faster than enrollment was being acquired. The Board was not being notified, much less asked for approval of this, or of the payment of higher salaries than originally budgeted. When queried, the Director would put off arguments by stating that this was a matter of professional judgment which the parents were not qualified as laymen to question. More and more, this theory, our lack of qualification, was to become the basis for undermining any role the Board could effectively play in the running of the school. The parents were becoming merely a rubber stamp of approval as the Director's actions brought him increasingly into conflict with us. One by one, members of the Board were also being divided from each other as the Director used the very potent power of his control over the children's fate, and the parents' fear, to keep the more questioning of us in line.

I was to lock horns with him personally one day when, in an official visit to the school, I conducted my business with him and was on my way out. We had been told we must not visit the classrooms as this was upsetting to the children. Any visit would have to be pre-arranged with parents under controlled circumstances.

So it was with my hands on the door and about to leave that I stopped, peered around and saw nobody in the hall. Feeling very much like a prying, interfering mother, but unable to control my earnest desire to see something of what was going on in the school, I peeked through the glassed-in section of the door of my son's classroom. No sign of any books. Jesse was sitting in a corner, rocking and peering out of the window. He looked completely out of it, off into some dream world of his own. Popcorn was scattered loosely all over the desks, which were grimy with dirt. Children were scattered all over the classroom, some playing with clay, others drawing, still others doing nothing at all. The teacher was smoking a cigarette and talking to an aide; all this at 9:30 in the morning. Surely this wasn't a lunch break.

Now I was looking into other classes, only to see similar scenes. No books, no sign of anything but art materials.

Suddenly a cold voice down the hall sent chills through me.

"What do you think you're doing?"

It was the assistant director, one of those additional people hired at an administrative salary against the injunctions of the Board, and she was ordering me out of the school.

"You are not permitted here now. Please leave," she was saying.

I felt like a common criminal, caught in the act of stealing. Stealing what, a look at my own child; a desire to know what teachers are doing with the children in my own school? Caught between wanting to run and finding an excuse for peeking, I hesitated, for something in her voice raised my hackles. She was speaking to me as if I was a child. She'd gone too far, and there was no longer a choice of meekly walking out without losing every vestige of self-respect. So I answered her, telling her she had no right to order me out. I demanded to speak to the Director.

Now the two of us were in his office, and it was hard to know which of us was more upset. The Director seemed to be enjoying the scene of two emotional women confronting each other, and it was apparent I had already lost the battle to keep my dignity. With a show of magnanimous courtesy, he gently reminded me of the rules, but apologized for the behavior of his assistant. It was then that I said the words which were to open the long war between us.

"I was not disturbing anyone in the classroom," I told him. "If the rules were made for this purpose, my actions were not deserving of such a reaction. Surely, there isn't anything to hide from the parents, is there?"

In the weeks that followed this incident, I tried to make peace with the Director. I went to the school to talk about Jesse's progress, thinking that if I appealed to him on the basis of my son's needs, the personality difficulties could be pushed into the background. After all, while he was at the school, a good relationship was in the best interests of my child's progress. Hopefully, he might start working on academics with Jesse, or open up an approach to more social contacts with his peer group. His language concepts were still very primitive, and also needed intensive remediation.

Starting with an apology for any discomfort I might have caused him, I asked how I could cooperate with him in his efforts to help Jesse, and what supportive work I could do at home. His answer told me where I stood.

"Whatever the original cause of Jesse's problems," he was saying, "they have been far outweighed by environmental factors at home. You have been destructive in your relationship with him, maintaining a symbiotic hold in which you have prevented him from developing as a separate individual. The destructive tendencies in you have gone too far at this point and Jesse will probably never achieve normalcy. The best you can do is to try to accept him as he is, and just give him love. Demand nothing else from him."

He was thrusting daggers into my heart with his textbook recital. Were a parent to take his words seriously, it could destroy any possibility of building communication between herself and her child. It could also destroy the parent as a human being. He was telling me that I was defective both as a parent and as a human being with a normal capacity for love; that I had crippled my child forever; that I was incompetent and incapable of maintaining a normal parent-child relationship.

"We are not planning on giving Jesse academics at this time," he continued, "because he isn't ready for it. His program consists of some perceptual work, lots of arts and crafts, and free expression between the teacher and him. It is essentially a therapeutic atmosphere in which Jesse can feel free to participate or not; where he can achieve emotional stability. If any discipline is needed in teaching him, it is best coming from us, not from you." He was going on and on with his dialectic, and all I could think of was, how wrong for Jesse; how little this man knew about Jesse's needs. Why was he trying to compensate for some imagined maltreatment on my part? Could he really believe this of me?

How much this man must hate me had begun to seep into my shocked mind. How easily he could crush me, if I believed him, for no conscience-stricken parent could withstand this kind of onslaught without deleterious effects on family relationships. Only the security gained from all those soul-searching years, and the knowledge I had gained along the way, enabled me to recognize this as a vicious attack at my vitals. Had I encountered this man much earlier in Jesse's life, when I was beleaguered with guilt and feelings that somehow I had caused his problems through neglect, his words might have shaken me to the core.

But now I felt, forewarned is forearmed. I must find out how far he would go with this story. Jesse must be protected, for an attack on me in the proper places would weaken the whole fabric of my relationship with the school district and prevent me from having an influence on his educational prerogatives. In the end, I was convinced, Jesse would suffer for it. With his pessimistic beliefs about Jesse's developmental stagnation, it would be a communication to the district that they needn't try too hard, for it would be of little use.

I had seen enough of this man and his kind of school to realize how dangerous he was to all the parents and children alike. His philosophy was one of antagonism to anyone with the label "parent." Every child in the school, regardless of diagnosis, was considered by him to be emotionally disturbed because of environmental deficits. I could recall a conversation during a business meeting when he made this philosophy plain to the assembled parents. We were sitting around waiting for the rest of the Board to appear.

"How is Stevie, these days, Mildred? Is the new medication helping him," one of the parents asked.

"I think so," Mildred said cheerfully. "He seems to be more in control of his emotions, a little less excitable. We did have one explosion, however, when his sister Judith ate the last piece of pie for dessert without saving him any. It took me fifteen minutes to calm him down."

"Well, the reaction may have been extreme, but perhaps he felt that she had been inconsiderate to him," the first parent replied.

"Oh, yes, she was, but you know, I explained over and over that I would bake more tomorrow and he could have two pieces. It was as though I couldn't make him understand what I was saying. He had to have it right then and there."

"Many of us have children like that, Mildred, impulsive, unable to plan for tomorrow, even for the next few hours. Time sequences seem to have little meaning for them. The medication may help him control his emotions, but of course it can't substitute for learning gaps," the first parent said kindly.

"Whatever it does, I'm glad for the crutch. His tantrums used to be continuous. I was ready to send him to residential school, he was so disruptive to the whole family. But I think the neurologist has finally found a good remedy," Mildred replied.

"It might not be such a bad idea," a new voice intervened, "to take Stevie out of the home situation." It was the Director, who had heard the whole conversation.

"What do you mean," Mildred said in bewilderment and hurt pride. "Just when things are better?"

"Well," he replied, "if I had my way, I would remove every child from the control of his parents."

Thus, the treatment at the school was to be non-academic, non-vocational; a therapeutic atmosphere in which the children were to be free to act out their emotional feelings. To say that he was not qualified technically to conduct such an undertaking merely skims the surface. This kind of philosophy assumes that the children in question could be integrated enough to sort out their feelings. Perhaps it was something he needed to do for himself, but our children were confused, disoriented, lacking the perceptual and cognitive integrity for organizing their behavior appropriately. This was his response to children who most needed someone who could structure their world and make them feel secure.

I was to see some disastrous results from his administration. I would learn about children being encouraged to hit each other, break equipment, eat their food like animals. Every cultural convention needed by them to make their way into acceptance by society was flouted.

So I brought these thoughts privately to the attention of the Board, only to meet with resistance. They, like me, were frightened by this man. But their fears for the school's existence were even greater. They could see no way for the school to survive without him. It had taken long enough to reach a point of stability with the county and the districts. How would they react to a change so soon in leadership? Where would we even find someone competent enough to take over the position? It would take two years for the Board to become convinced, and only as the abuses grew worse, that whatever the outcome, we could not continue under his direction. Only then would we embark on a search for a new director, and our efforts would be rewarded.

In the meantime, the house of cards came tumbling down on other Board members' heads. One by one, they learned of reports sent to school authorities damaging to their reputation, both as Trustees of the school and as wholesome, loving parents. Malicious stories were spread about the school being 'in the red' because of our meddling. Damaging reports labeling children as psychotic, and in one case, as a pyromaniac, were sent to the districts of those children whose parents annoyed him. It began with other children not related to Board members. Dismissals occurred summarily with no notice to the Board. In some cases, as he admitted to a parent in a rare moment of candor, it was because he or one of the teachers didn't like a child; in others, it was the parent he disliked. Always a report damaging to the child was the reason for dismissal. At times the parents, too, would receive character assassination in these reports. Even those staff members not attuned to him were accused of behavior damaging to their professional reputation. No one was immune from slander.

Complaints from parents and staff came flooding in to the paralyzed Board, which felt helpless to do anything about them because of the necessity for confrontation with the Director. Just the attempt to keep the school in running condition took up all of our energy resources, leaving us drained after every Board meeting. And so it continued for two years. Some school districts during this time, realizing that children they had sent were receiving no education, withdrew them. Others, having no other place for the children, closed their eyes, or perhaps, were convinced by the Director's reports that this was the proper environment for them. Still other school districts would refer only those children who were unable to be placed anywhere else because of their destructive or severe behavior patterns.

I was not to learn about the damaging things stated about Jesse and me until much later. All information sent to the school district was labeled "confidential" by the Director which, under the existing state law of the time, meant that the parent could not see the report. He or she might only have it interpreted by an appropriate professional. Fortunately, I had a long history of good relationships in my school district and community. It was to help neutralize the effects of slanderous assaults.

For those other parents and staff, whose children and reputations have suffered at the hands of this man, we must always feel a measure of grief and guilt.

They had no recourse to the Board, and they should have. At least one child was institutionalized after being dropped from the school because his mother, alone and without resources, could not care for him. One other child could not be placed again for another whole year when the label "pyromaniac" was attached to his record for the first time in his life. What had really happened in this latter case was a matter of gross negligence on the part of staff. He and another child had picked up some matches carelessly left around by a teacher (who, remember, was allowed to smoke in the classroom!). She was also unaware that they had walked out of the school into the woods, where the other child, not the boy eventually labeled, lit the matches.

Then there was Billy, the lost Billy, whose memory haunts me always.

He was the oldest child in the school, and had suffered most from bureaucratic negligence. He had been moved around, like checkers on a board, into different classes, in and out of his home district. He had also spent some years at home with little or no instruction, and in general had received very little consistent educational planning in the course of his fourteen years of life. His parents, patient and enduring, had very limited financial means to help fill in the gaps for Billy. And so, here he was, an awkward youngster, tall for his age, with some promise, in spite of time's cruel impediments, of doing well with vocational training. But he had a flaw which was fatal in our environment. He was too gentle, somewhat effeminate in manner, and not young enough or small enough to still be considered "cute." The teachers didn't like him, and an excuse was found to expel him half-way through his first year at school.

Now began the final ordeal for his parents. After a long hassle with the state over their legal rights, Billy was placed in a school far away from home. Yet he learned to travel there through public transportation, get off at the appropriate stop, and walk, by himself, the rest of the way to the school. Billy walked, all right, into a pit. For amongst the school population were some socially maladjusted boys, young toughs, who seized upon his vulnerable personality and brutalized him. Almost overnight, the effects became evident. The gentle, effeminate boy became a violent, foul-mouthed terror to the whole family. They sought out psychiatric help, but to no avail. Love turned into fear, and fear into despair.

Billy was put into a state institution. *Dear God, suffer thy little children....*

POWER PLAYS AT SCHOOL

As the many tales of woe poured into us during that first year of operation, the Board increasingly became a ghost crew, watching numbly or murmuring ineffectually while every vestige of control was wrested from us.

Item: Agreement in By-Laws and Board minutes that staff and children not be dismissed without knowledge and consent of the Board; disregarded.

Item: Agreement in By-Laws and minutes that teachers' qualifications and contracts be discussed with the Board; ignored.

Item: Agreement that the parent group plan open school meetings with the goal of inviting other professionals in the field to speak; nullified by direct interception of the Director.

Item: Vouchers for monies required—none; explanation for such expenditures—"professional judgment".

Meetings became increasingly tense. There we all sat, like nervous children, wondering what he would pull on us next. Walking into the meeting room, silently taking our seats, with barely a nod to each other, grimness walked in with us. A grim atmosphere as the author of grim tidings himself, Mr. Grimlad, we shall call him, made his appearance.

People begin entering the room, slowly filtering in, sinking into their seats, men and women, all sizes and shapes, from all walks of life, their faces pale, serious.

There is Bill, tall, white-haired, distinguished looking, a lawyer by profession.

And Henry, small, frail-looking, a pediatrician.

Then there's Mildred, sweet-voiced, gentle, a perpetually frightened look in her eyes.

Rosemary has just entered, walking with quick, firm stride, a business woman's air of decisiveness about her.

Is there something about them, as I searched each face, each one's bodily carriage, that can give some tell-tale clue to the observer, some singular aspect they all share beneath their disparities, which marks them as bearers of misfortune in the shape of a child? Is there some long-forgotten sin which has sealed their fate, made a mockery of their love, useless the struggle for their children? Perhaps there is some flaw in their physical appearance one can pick up if one is sharp, or something in their character, surely, that accounts for their common tragedy?

Grimlad took his seat. He was greeted perfunctorily. Some even made an attempt at pleasantries as though to delay somehow the heavy hours to come.

The meeting is called to order. Bills for supplies and equipment are presented. There is a new and expensive typewriter, additional office equipment. Board members look at the costs, dismayed.

"Where is the money coming from to pay for these items," one member asks. *"We haven't budgeted for them, in view of the fact that your typewriter and office equipment were considered perfectly satisfactory.*

"We can pay for them on the installment plan, and take the monies from the classroom supplies item. I won't need any for awhile. I consider these office supplies important."

"You've already purchased them"

"Yes."

"You know, we haven't approved any of this, and you are obligated to receive approval for expenses this large."

"I will not submit to having my hands tied by members of the Board all the time. The smooth flow of school business requires more freedom." There is an angry edge to his voice.

"What is this I see about the hiring of another school psychologist? I thought we approved of Mr.—last month, and now I find you've hired someone we haven't met or heard about. What happened to the first man"

"I found him unsatisfactory. You will have to rely on my professional judgment about that."

"According to our contract, applications and resumes are supposed to be submitted to us. Where are they?"

"They're superfluous. I have reviewed all the pertinent information and found everything satisfactory. The information is rather technical for a lay Board and therefore of little value to you."

Heated debate ensues. Hal demands that the By-Laws and school regulations be followed.

"We will be the judge of what is too technical for us to understand," he says indignantly. *"This matter will have to be tabled until the Board has approved the new applicant."*

Grimlad turns steel-cold eyes on him.

"If you cannot allow me to run the school as I deem proper, then perhaps you should look for another Director. I can leave anytime, and I doubt if my staff will want to remain without me." (What is he saying? Is he ready to close down the school?)

"You know, Hal," he continues, *"You have been very antagonistic to me. It's very hard for me to go from meetings like this to working with your child the next day, without ill effects. My feelings toward the parent must be reflected in my attitude toward the child."*

The pulse quickened in Hal and myself. I stared wide-eyed at him. Ah! So now it's blackmail. Jesse's fate hangs in the balance if we don't behave, he's saying. The meeting droned on, item after item. There would be some weak protests, but the message had been received by all. Only once did the Board show strong unity during that miserable year. Grimlad went one step too far by offering to buy the school from us and relieve us of the "burden". On this we were all stimulated to action. Never! That would surely mean the end of the road for many of the Trustees' children. Who could then be sure of his child's continued attendance? And where would the children's road lead after he had banished them?

How many times I was to think back to those dark days of despair. How could all of us, intelligent, sensible people, have allowed ourselves to become so victimized by someone we all knew in the depths of our souls was creating unnecessary havoc in our lives. I have thought back also to those midnight sessions in an all-night diner, after bleak Board meetings, when I and my huddled band would sit together, pour out our frustrations to each other, comfort each other as much as possible. We'd plan those endless futile attempts to recover possession of our faculties the next time, always one step behind as we planned for that next time, always amazed at the course of events each of those "next times" brought. The mountains of calories we all consumed at that midnight hour, the bad jokes we all told, just to bring some relief and warmth to our frozen souls. I can never forget them, this small band of people with whom I shared so much grief, and to whom I felt so close.

The second year was to be an intensification of the first. With more children in the school, Mr. Grimlad was to poison the minds of the newer parents against the Board in an attempt to take over control of the school. We would meet a diverse group of parents that year, and feel and see how outcast people can become as a result of their children's problems; how mentally crippling such problems can be for people who haven't the physical or mental resources to cope with them. Among this new group we would find people who were peculiarly suited to the philosophy of a Grimlad: people who wished to be told that they were bad parents, who needed to believe, masochistically, that they were responsible for their child's illness (*illness, not condition*), and not some accident of nature. Such people had never worked out their own guilt complexes.

Then there were people who did not want to cope with their child's problems or could not because of an overload of family woes. These people welcomed the advice to attempt no home training, simply give the child love and leave the rest to the school. There were parents who knew nothing about the school's beginnings, the composition of the Board, the financial risks we had undertaken, or our dissatisfaction with Grimlad. These people were patronized by the Director, subtly bribed with stories of what he could do for their children. For the most part, they were people whose children had been neglected, who themselves lacked the background to deal effectively with their difficulties, and who could be easily swayed by a literate, clever man such as Grimlad.

By this time in the second year of operation, the Board was reasonably united on the need to search for a new Director. Now began the climax of the ordeal. We searched all that year and found, amazingly, that the position of Director of our school was a sought-after prize, for it was a position in which a responsible, ambitious young man or woman would have much opportunity to put into practice good educational programs. It was a position that commanded respect from colleagues in the field, and to the degree of his or her success with the school, his or her own career would be enhanced. We spoke to many candidates and I visited a school where one of them worked. We were very favorably impressed with her and got excellent references, both about her character and her wide experience of achievement with many diverse kinds of children.

Despite all the precautions of secrecy about our search in order to prevent Grimlad's irritation from being vented on the children, word of what we were doing reached him. This brought an intensified effort on his part to divest us of the school. Districts were told that the present school was going bankrupt because of the Board's incompetence and would not be in operation the following year. County officials were enlisted in Grimlad's support. Parents of the school were divided into factions favoring one side or another.

A Board meeting was called to discuss the contract of employment for the following year, Hal presiding as President. The unavowed purpose of the Board was to fire the Director and hire a new one already reviewed and approved by a majority of members. In approving our candidate, a far wiser Board had sought and received the guidance of well-respected professionals in its search and had taken great care to review all credentials of the candidate. The Director, however, had once again outsmarted the Board by bringing in county officials, parents who would support him, and staff who would speak to his good work. At what was to be a private business meeting, we were held up to scorn, ridiculed as we attempted to state the long, factual case for non-renewal. The meeting turned into a circus with accusations flying, demands made, and disorder rampant; after many long hours it was adjourned by the President without any of its purposes accomplished.

Hal and I went home that night in a state of collapse. We each looked at the haggard face of the other and hoped the strain would not be too much for our mental faculties. I had lost a lot of weight over the past two years. Friends had expressed concern about my appearance. We were both at our weakest ebb, with Hal taking the brunt of the punches as President of the Board. That night Hal secretly hid the sleeping pills contained in the medicine cabinet. He had looked into my face and seen a distraught, almost wild look, and for the first time in our marriage, was unsure of my state of mind.

Somehow in the next several weeks, with the help of legal advice, the Board managed to convene the necessary meeting. In contrast to the former one, a dry, unemotional vote was called in which the majority of the Board voted non-renewal of the present Director and approved the new candidate. The matter, however, would not end there. Grimlad attempted to convince the church fathers that he should be given the operation of the premises for the following year, telling them that he was starting his own school because of an intractable and emotionally unstable Board which was hampering him. When it appeared that his wish would be granted, our group asked for and received an opportunity to be heard. After hearing both sides, and seeing documentation from us, the church fathers decided to award the parents continued use of their facilities. A very large victory indeed, since the school was certified for the present quarters, making our new beginning a little easier.

There were some more hard knocks before this was to be, however, for Grimlad fought hard to the very end. And so, as the last day of the school year came, and in spite of an agreement to hold each other harmless and leave all school materials intact, it was discovered that we had the keys to empty drawers and files. He had removed all the school records and most of the equipment purchased with school funds! Everything we needed to continue operation was gone. We would have to begin the new term with larger outlays of money for new school supplies, convince districts to return children's records to a school they thought was defunct, and at the same time, convey to Grimlad that any further sabotage would result in a costly law suit which neither he nor we could afford.

Amazingly, these last blows were weathered by a battle-toughened group, who at last had stood up and fought back. The victory was the children's, for now we were to have a good, dedicated Director who would bring the school, and our lives, out into the sunshine. Sadly, however, our numbers were diminished. Some of our people had had enough, and would not be returning to the school.

8

A SPECIAL BOND

The next five years of Jesse's life were to be a period of stability and growth. He had lost two whole years, vital years for him. He had made some gains in language and social concepts, but those gains were more likely due to maturation factors than to any educational intervention.

What little academic work he had in those years had been supplied by me, with the advice of a professional friend, who had guided me in my work with him. It had been very rough, trying to be a teacher and a mother at the same time. There was little relief from the constant tension, and the emotions of a mother were always interfering with the objectivity of a teacher.

The first year under the new Director was not to bring a whole lot of relief for me. Unseasoned in her role and new to the state with all its political machinery, she would have her troubles just trying to keep the ship afloat after the battering it had incurred, and new storms were on the horizon. Jesse was also unlucky enough to have a holdover from the previous year's staff teaching him, one who had been too imbued with Grimlad's brand of philosophy to give him the academic work he needed.

But a new spirit was coming. A young man in Jesse's summer camp program would turn out to be an ideal teacher for him over the next two years. Through their relationship, Jesse would blossom out into a sweet, happy boy. Looking back at the reports from school in those years, they indicate a mixed picture, a strange concoction that made me both hopeful and dejected at the same time. Puzzling words that described profound disabilities, yet an intuitive belief on the part of teachers and therapists that there were innate qualities locked up within this bewildering child. It had always been that way. When would the pieces begin to fit, the picture become clearer, I wondered.

Brain damage had been the first medical report; a structural defect of the central nervous system present at birth or before, resulting in severe functional defects, particularly in sensory perception and language.

But the pediatrician had seen an alertness and thought he had more intelligence than was apparent at that stage.

Then, in his first year of formal school, his teachers were reporting progress in learning to do perceptual tasks, such as matching forms, distinguishing colors by name, responding to spatial orientation such as up, down, under, in front of. They would say hopeful words about him: "Developmental lag," one would tell me, as though maturation of the nervous system would mean greater learning capacity. Always, however, he was being tested in comparison to his normal peers, with those infernal IQ tests that were really designed for testing normally-functioning children only. Always, it was a depressing picture when compared with others of his chronological age.

No matter that with initiation of formalized instruction he was making steady progress. He had not been able to pick up cues from his environment the way a normal toddler does, or learn from his mother's lap as other children do long before their formal school years, and he was consequently far behind. Nor could he learn at an accelerated pace, so that he would always lag behind.

Then came those two terrible years under Grimlad, with no structured learning, and he lost more time. Precious sands of time that can never be recovered, as I saw it. For it is a common phenomenon among mothers of children with developmental disabilities to be frantic about feeding in to their children all the mental stimulation possible. No matter what we are told about our children's potential, we are in a hurry against time. Call it denial; I call it optimism. It is the root upon which we fight for the best that can be offered to our children. We may have to temper it with reality at some time in the future. But we will know that we have given our special children every opportunity, and who is so prescient that he can know with certainty what is the eventual potential for any individual child?

It has been said that a child learns more in the first few years of his life than he will ever learn in any similar period of time for the rest of his life. How much greater then is the loss of that time for a child like Jesse. The doctors did not see those years as urgently important for they never seemed impressed with the necessity for early education. But educators would not agree with them. Today there is a diametrically different view about the need for early stimulation. A whole new movement was to begin in later years for early identification and remediation at a preschool age. Federal grants have been used to start just such programs, and legislatures are frequently pressured to provide the necessary funding for more such programs. Too late for Jesse.

I learned of a summer camp remediation program being run by a nearby college. It was mainly for the benefit of training students who would staff the camp, but the proximity to those halls of learning might open up new approaches for teaching Jesse, I thought, and I was excited by the possibility. And so, at the end of the term I registered Jesse in the program. That summer, Jesse met Nick, one of the teachers at the camp, a fateful meeting, for Nick was to become a teacher at our school and Jesse's beloved companion over the next two years.

The reports at summer's end had been pretty somber. No coordination, or demonstrable ability to organize his faculties, no ability to concentrate on a task ... no ... no ... no, negatives in super-abundance. They did feel he was aware of his surroundings, yet unable to organize them into a meaningful structure. Little useful language at first, they said, but with some improvement over time in the use of simple sentences.

Back in school that autumn, Jesse sat in a corner, rocking, clutching a toy. He had shut himself off from the other children. Even on a one-to-one basis, he would phase in and out. He was a withdrawn child, an unhappy little boy who would not be able to learn until he was brought back to the real world. Oh, those two years when this behavior was encouraged! But Nick would not let this continue. Facing him, cupping his chin and making Jesse look at him, he would have him repeat names of objects, then praise him, hugging him and rough-housing with him, which Jesse loved, providing the physical contact that was so good for him.

At first, he would only repeat what Nick said.

"Say car, Jesse, say car."

"Say car, Jesse, say car," Jesse repeated.

Patiently, Nick tried again. Holding up pictures, he said, "Say house, Jesse, say house."

"House," Jesse said.

"Good, Jesse," then a quick hug. Jesse smiled happily.

"Now name all of these pictures. What's this?"

"Lamp."

"And this?"

"Bottle of milk."

And so on, finally giving him his reward, a piece of candy and a big hug. But it was the hug and the praise that really worked, showing Jesse in a way nothing else could that he was loved and that his efforts were appreciated. Nick's feelings were different from the teachers under Grimlad. They had pitied Jesse, expected nothing from him, and got nothing. Nick expected, demanded, keeping up an intense barrage that was tempered only by love. And Jesse responded. The shell was cracking. He was becoming a happy boy again. Now he was more interested in everything around him, happy to play purposeful games as long as he knew what to do. He was also learning to read, through phonetics, the one-word nouns that named the pictures Nick held up. This would progress to short sentences, and then to short stories.

Jesse was also developing a sense of humor. He would purposely pick up the wrong object in response to Nick's question, then look up at him with smiling eyes. When Nick showed frustration, he would laugh out loud and hand him the correct object. His sense of humor was even more subtle at times. If he saw two children in the class accidentally bump into each other, this was funny; once when a teacher was looking for something, only to find it right in front of her, Jesse laughed delightedly. Nothing that went on in the room escaped his notice. I seized on these events as a sign of greater ability than was apparent on the surface. Perhaps I was exaggerating their importance, but here at least, he seemed to be ordering his environment appropriately.

The sense of humor was to develop in sophistication. Jesse would watch a movie intended for grown-ups, see a subtly humorous event and understand it intuitively in a way most children his age would miss. One could see that it registered by his reaction. Somewhere, in his neurological development, there seemed to be an intact non-verbal modality which was operating at a higher level.

Something else was to happen that would bring greater understanding with it than usual for a child his age, this one a sad event—his beloved grandmother died. We took Jesse and our other two children to the funeral, for we did not want them shielded from life, neither the happy nor the sad events that everyone faces. We had never explained to Jesse about death, for we felt sure he would not understand. But something had been, strangely, communicated to him. Even when Lynn and Andrew found it difficult to believe that Grandma would never return for a visit again, even when Hal and I were having difficulty accepting this idea, Jesse had made the adjustment.

I asked him, tentatively, one day several months later, "Where is Grandma Betty?"

"She's dead," he answered.

Okay, so he knows the word, I thought, but he can't really know what that means. So I asked the next question.

"Will she come and see us?"

The answer was a quick. "No."

And he really did understand, for he never asked for her again. Yet in life, she had been constantly on his mind, knowing he would get a toy from her each time she visited. How well, I wonder, do other seven-year-old children accept this concept? There was to be a generalization from this concept which also surprised me. Jesse began asking questions about his own death.

"Will Jesse die?" he would ask.

"Not for a long time," I answered tremulously.

"After a long time you die?" (The "you" a reversed pronoun meaning himself). "Yes."

"Tomorrow after a long time you die?"

"No, no. We all expect to live much longer, Jesse. Everyone has to die sometime: Mommy, Daddy, Lynn and Andrew."

But this answer made matters worse, for now Jesse really felt abandoned. His fears were to continue long after, and the question would be asked frequently, for his understanding of time was very limited. He could understand yesterday, today, and tomorrow, but after that, it was hazy. Then he wanted to know where people go after they die.

"To heaven," I answered, helpless to explain more.

"You can't come back from heaven!" he would say, exploding into anger and frenzied fear. His teachers would hear it, too,

"You can't come back to school after you die?" he would ask.

How could we make him understand; how could we soothe his fears when he didn't understand what a long time is, I wondered. I showed him pictures of old people, pointed them out on the street, trying to demonstrate that one usually grows old before dying. I talked about Grandma's age. Gradually, the fears subsided, but only into the subconscious. For now he had to sleep with his door open, and have a night light on.

Jesse continued to show improvement at school. He still tended to daydream at times, but his attention span was increasing. He was beginning to read with comprehension. Expressive language was greatly improved and he was formulating original sentences to express his desires. They had also started on a physical therapy regimen of weight bearing and coordination exercises. He enjoyed basketball and gym activities with other children. Reliance on adults, however, was still considerable—he could not initiate activities on his own. And so it went: a mixed picture of a child trying to make his way into acceptance by society.

Nick and I had many conferences. It was the friendly relationship of two people respectful of each other and pulling in the same direction. I was welcome at the school whenever I wished to come. It wasn't even necessary to call first! Somehow, with the pressure off, I no longer had as much need to drop in at the school, maybe because I knew what was going on there. Contact with everyone who saw Jesse was continuous and two-way, with frequent notes back and forth about school and home activities. At last the whole child was being put together, piece by piece.

In the following year, Jesse was to increase his vocabulary, his reading skills, and some simple arithmetic concepts. He would also continue to have a limited understanding of his environment, needing to be formally taught about things like the sun, soil, seasons, etc. Concept formation would be very difficult, but once he understood, he could generalize to other circumstances, the way he did when his Grandma died.

The new atmosphere at the school was a complete reversal of the preceding one. Instead of relying on emotions and intuition, education was looked at as a behavioral science. Every facet of the child was to be described in accurate behavioral terms, with individual goals prescribed and progress monitored on a continuous basis. Detailed descriptions of where the child was and step-by-step progress were always forthcoming to the parents, so that they might better understand their own child's abilities and disabilities. In some cases, home training programs were offered to parents in order to carry the smooth progression home. The parent, in other words, was a full partner in her son's or daughter's education, if she wished to be.

Yet, through the neat pattern of detailed reports and educational verbiage ran a thread of another color. The thing that had both frustrated and provided hope to Jesse's mama and papa was doing likewise to his teachers. He fit into no neat categories. Always, they could feel the picture was more complex, that there was more inside Jesse than he was giving out. Less dedicated teachers might not have seen this. It is always tempting to categorize, to fit people into neat little patterns so that we may have the comfort of planning without too many discomfiting surprises. It provides us with a security blanket. It also provides limited expectations.

Jesse's teachers were always searching, always trying to extend the limits. Much of it was frustrating, but every once in a while, some bright little light shone through, giving them heart for the next effort. So there would be no quick answers.

And then there was that sweet little personality that caught everyone's affection. For Jesse was gentle, affectionate, anxious to please, responsive. Try as they might to describe him in scientific, objective terms, this would catch them off guard. It may have played no small role in their optimistic attitude toward him. Long may it be so. May we never fully understand in clinical terms that wonderful something in human beings that we call the soul. If that is advice well taken, however, it is not advice I always took myself. There were to be many weak moments when I needed that security blanket of categorizing Jesse.

On one such occasion, impatient to wait out time's answers, day by day, year by year, I repeated my foolishness of the past and sought out another psychiatrist for a prognosis. It was during that first year of the new school regime when I still felt somewhat in limbo. As Hal and I walked into the doctor's office with Jesse, the usual silly thoughts ran through my head. Would the doctor know how far Jesse could go in his school career? What kind of work would he be able to do? Would he live independently as a man?

The doctor greeted us, telling us to wait in the anteroom while he saw Jesse. I watched as Jesse walked through the open door into the doctor's office. Then Jesse let me know how he felt about my doubts, about my need to test him. To my horror, he walked straight through the office, past the doctor as if he didn't see him, to the far corner of the room, where he stood stiffly, facing the wall. The door closed, and with it, a door in my heart. We sat there, biting our nails. Alternately we paced, like nervous parents waiting to be told the baby will live.

At last we were called in for a conference. With Jesse sitting in the chair, staring blankly at nothing, the doctor began to talk, ignoring the child's presence with his words. "Jesse is profoundly retarded," he stated. "We must not expect him to learn much beyond a kindergarten to third grade level. He can live at home with you as long as he is not disturbing to the rest of the family, but otherwise …"

Hal had to help me out to the car. When I had recovered my composure, I felt anger: anger at the doctor, anger at Jesse for not cooperating, even anger at Hal for not sharing in my diatribes against the doctor. No more prognoses, never again! Jesse would go for medical checkups, and occasional neurological review, which is required by the school district, but that's all.

9

UNFORESEEN PATHWAYS

It has been said that we pass through several stages of life from the cradle to the grave, each with its own promise and crisis, each bringing new maturity, like a new layer of skin.

For many, perhaps this is true. Implied in this concept, however, is the image of someone whose core form is recognizable through the progression of years, in which the older person can still identify with some part of his younger self. Implied is a change so gradual, a transition so smooth as to keep in touch with our past lives. Such is the stuff of reminiscence and nostalgia, family reunions and picture albums. It embodies our desire not to get too far away from our true essence. For others, this is inadequate to describe what has happened to them. They have been metamorphosed from one form into a completely new one, each unrecognizable to the other. Among the more fortunate, this may come about without too much trauma destroying the whole being in its wake, leaving a foundation for growth and stability.

I was becoming a different woman. Some would call it maturity, but maturity doesn't happen merely as the product of additional years. It was an outgrowth of deep experience; it was a result of constant search for meaningfulness in the face of confusion. Part of it had to be the result of being buffeted, at least a little, but not being submerged by the blows. One must struggle to the surface by his own efforts and be able to find some relief before going onward—a kind of homeostasis, as it were. Looking back at old snapshots, old memories, it is hard to believe that the smiling woman in the picture is not someone else. Looking at her is like looking at a snapshot of a childhood friend with all the curiosity and regret one feels over a parting of the ways. I was a mother to that naïve child-woman, or so it seemed to me then.

The progression had not been smooth or gradual. Life, as I thought about it at the time this account was written, had always unfolded in a series of jerks and bumps from my early, somewhat unhappy but protected childhood, to my early marriage with its transience during Hal's army days; then the later business moves, the unsettledness as well as the excitement of those years. Then came young motherhood, with all its hopes and dreams. So far, not too hard to see the transitions, to relate with the earlier girl. Finally, the plunge into new waters. The trauma; the years of crisis; the isolation from the kinds of people I knew and was a part of; new political realities, old unrealized needs; and soon, the dreams are gone, the ties with the past shattered. I was mobilized into action, and I hardly noticed the changes as the years passed—until one day I realized I had been torn so completely from those early roots that they were not recognizable. This is the moment we begin to question who we are and where we are going; the beginning of a search for meaningfulness. This is either the moment for strength of purpose or resignation to chaos. We either change ourselves to meet the new demands, or retreat from the world.

Once, long ago, the serious questions involved political issues, how one stood on social welfare, education, feeding under-developed nations. We attended bright, witty parties, argued the serious questions with other bright, concerned people. Our lives stretched out before us neatly and I could envision all of us as humane contributors to man's welfare. We would make our mark in the world and leave something beneficial behind us.

The serious questions were closer to home now, and much less grandiose. I would be happy if I could just contribute to my children's welfare. Others would have to find answers for themselves to the other questions. My thoughts were on Jesse's needs, and the loneliness of youngsters like him. There seemed such a void in our lives because of this. It was reflected in the beating we allowed ourselves to take during the first years of the school. Would any of the parent group have had to suffer so much abuse at the hands of unscrupulous people had there been appropriate facilities for our children? Would any of us have been so vulnerable if there had been psychological counseling or better understanding within the community of our needs, or the educational directions available to us?

It was clear that parents in the community had to organize with the hope that this would provide a means to bring new awareness within the community. Other resources could be provided through our union, such as recreation. Jesse needed to play with other children after school. It was as important to his growth as it is to other children. Think of an average child coming home and sitting in his room without ever seeing other children after school. He didn't have Boy Scouts, or Little League, or any of the usual social and recreational outlets provided in most communities. He couldn't run down the street to join in games with other children. His day ended when school was over.

A group of us met to discuss these matters. I did a lot of talking also to educators, service clubs and governing councils about the children's recreational needs. We also wanted to see more classes opened within the community setting. After all, we were not in the business of maintaining a private school. The Board, even the Director, would have been happy to phase out the school if classes opened up within each of the school districts for children who would otherwise sit home or become wards of the state.

Experience has shown that to the extent children are shunted out of their communities to other placement, to that extent does the community wash its hands of them. Unseen, unfelt as part of their own community, they had no place in it. Good as our school was now, it must still be considered a hothouse environment that bears little relationship to the real world. These children had to learn to emulate their normal peers. Even more importantly, the normal peer group had to learn to accept them. Perhaps then we could stop dichotomizing children as normal or abnormal, for most of our children still fall within a very large spectrum of behavior that can be seen as the ways of children. The community must come to see them, feel their presence, and provide for them, I thought, just as it does for its other citizens. Jesse was a non-visible shadow resident, who went off to a school away from everyone else, and came home, to remain away from everyone else. Even now, many years later, it is an ever-present concern for most communities have not recognized their responsibilities. Today, as ever, many of our children lead isolated lives. And yet, this situation can be a double-edged sword, for the alternative in recent years is frequently to place them in a mainstream public school, but without the additional funding for their social needs. Unlike other children, social training for children like Jesse requires formal processes, for what good is an education without the ability to relate to people.

With our new organization, we achieved temporary relief. Local town councils in surrounding communities were persuaded to donate some nominal funds, token amounts at best, toward a regional recreation program. We gathered all those children whose parents were willing to transport them into a school setting for extra-curricular activities. Along the way we met some beautiful people, special educators who still had energy after their day at school to give the children classes in home economics, woodworking, crafts and gym in an atmosphere in which socialization as well as practical skills were emphasized. Volunteers in the program included many high school students, who to our delight, showed a natural aptitude for communication with the children. They provided a joyful experience for us, and in appreciation we instituted a formal ceremony at their school graduations to give them the peer recognition they deserved.

But each year was a new struggle, for it meant once again asking for funds and hoping we could get enough to support our programs, find teachers, look for new school facilities as schedules changed, provide legal forms, insurance forms, and so on. It was a wearying task.

We move in our lives from task to task, in this way battening down the hatches, securing portholes, protecting our families and providing for them, planning for them, until they are able to fend for themselves. And while the storms raged outside, while I was busy keeping the good ship afloat, I paid little heed to the inner storms, and to time passing by. Many women move through their lives this way, vaguely uncomfortable about something they're not heeding, some inner need not being satisfied. It is only when the last child is off on his own, perhaps, when her energies are no longer being called for or desired as the mother protector, the safe harbor, the mover and planner of events, that her own personal crisis may become apparent.

Men, too, of course, may reach this crisis stage, perhaps a little earlier than women, for theirs is tied up with personal ambitions and reaching their peak of dynamic activity. They are likely to have faced their individual needs over a longer period of time, and will rebel sooner against the diminishing of creative strength, while mother is still enmeshed in her creative family role, subduing her inchoate self-needs. This is still true today, even though due to the rise in feminine consciousness women have become more aware of their own needs as individuals than they were in generations past. But today more women are also in the work force than ever before, adding to their role as homemaker, and this may also serve to divert attention from individual needs.

If such be the case, then I was putting off this time of crisis. The signals were there, and could be seen in the constant search for meaning. The seeking of a role, whether in community affairs, or in establishing the parent organization for recreation and social events in which my son could participate; then flinging off those roles in favor of a return to school for a new career, which I was soon to do, only to abandon that too: all were distress signals. Some find a satisfactory answer as they thrash about, the one role that fulfills their personal needs; others do not. Such thoughts flitted through my mind from time to time but could not remain long, for there was still too much insecurity in my role as a mother, and my energies were needed there. I was also conscious of needing reserves for my husband, whose love was my greatest source of support.

It was only to be in later years that I would face the ways my personal crisis had been avoided, sidetracked by the necessity to be there for Jesse and my family. I was to recognize later, too, what role the crisis played in the vulnerabilities that plagued me: things like the excessive guilt-feelings I harbored, and the need to escape from family problems. This type of situation tends to become a vicious cycle in which the more insecure I felt about myself, the more intensely involved I became in Jesse's affairs and to a lesser extent, in those of my other two children. This in turn allowed me to put off facing issues about myself and who I was as an individual. But I was sensing something wrong in the family structure, something for which I felt responsible. So intense had been my involvement with Jesse that I wondered what effects it would have on the rest of the family. Then, too, such intensity meant a loss of perspective and of balance. I had to talk with other parents, perhaps with a psychologist trained in parent counseling.

I had seldom been able to talk to other people about my children in the customary way most parents seek these outlets. Never underrate the value of the common coffee klatch; it is as necessary to good parenting as other forms of advice. Another balance tool that had been lost to me was the opportunity most parents have to see their children's interaction with peers, to guide them in their social relationships, and so develop the social being who will become the well-adjusted citizen. Jesse was still an island unto himself, with our recreation program only a token of what he needed. It was necessarily teacher-directed, heavily structured, lacking in those informal social improvisations that tell so much about the child and helps him to grow.

My daily problems seemed enormous and I wondered if other parents like me had similar ones, or could cope better with them. I also needed feedback on what the future might realistically look like for Jesse, which parents with older children like him might provide. There is so much written for the average parent and talked over in seminars and lectures through which they are fed constant information about their children's growing-up years and what to expect at each stage of development, but so little for us beyond an occasional conference. It was not a final, dead-end prognosis such as that provided by the last psychiatrist that I needed, but practical advice that would help me structure the environment for whatever growth potential there could be; a pro-active attitude, in other words, rather than a defeatist attitude. Every parent, no matter what the course for her child, needs to have this kind of advice.

Just being able to talk with people who I knew understood and were empathetic meant much for my peace of mind. It wasn't only professionals I needed to talk to; it was a good old-fashioned rap session I needed as well. Apparently other parents were feeling this need too, because the idea was greeted enthusiastically. Once before I could recall finding a small group like this, but that was when Jesse was very young and helpful as it was then, the problems were very different now.

I was concerned over the fact that he was maturing physically and I was fearful of new crises during his adolescent years. It was important to plan for them now. Some of the parents in the school had children already into their adolescence and they might be helpful, I thought. So there I was, meeting again with some of that old gang of mine, only this time under different circumstances, with none of the panic of former times.

Concerned parents assembled in a room with a psychologist who would monitor, but not otherwise intercept, the conversation. He could be there for information when asked, or to help us find additional outlets as needed. I looked at these people and I saw varying kinds of emotional adjustment mirrored in their faces. One mother seemed bewildered but passively accepting of fate. Another seemed quite confident and serene, almost as though she'd solved all her problems. Many of the fathers seemed to have taken on a supportive, but less involved role, leaving most of the decisions to their wives. But then, isn't that true of many families having only the usual concerns of raising children? Isn't it really the mother who faces the daily problems, makes the daily decisions that build up into the dominant role of raising the children? (Today in many families, fathers are more involved; yet I do not see mothers being relieved of the dominant role). How much more then is the mother's burden with a child such as ours? Two of the couples had more than one child in the family with developmental and emotional disabilities. How did they keep from running away, I wondered.

The group started off awkwardly, hesitantly at first. We who had spent all those desperate hours together at another time suddenly found ourselves vulnerable to each other. Now the subject matter came closer to the inner core. Talking about things that had been bottled up for so long, bringing into the open the complexity of guilt, fear and shame that had been hidden from the outside world in a self-protective vault until the hidden places had even become a comfortable adjustment; to uncover them now was like tearing off the scar that covers a festering but pain-dulled wound. We were to only partially succeed in uncovering insecurities, feelings of inadequacy, and the hidden depths of troubled minds.

I didn't tell them, for example, about that death wish I once harbored for Jesse (was it all gone by that time, I wonder?), or the involvement I sought with outside organizations while neglecting my internal obligations toward Jesse.

The group started by talking about mundane matters, the daily routines of our households, how each child participated in whatever ways he or she could. Listening to all of us, one would think this was just another coffee klatch of mothers and fathers who had everything under control, thank you; willing, of course, to give advice and be helpful to others. It was the outer shell talking, the one we had learned to present to the rest of the world, but was it necessary here? The more bewildered parents, those who had long ceased to fight, did less talking than the others. They had come along, perhaps out of a sense of obligation, but in essence, had become disengaged.

Gradually, chinks in the armor would show up. I would learn about children who had gotten into adolescence with no sense of identity. Theirs was not an identity crisis, as is customarily the adolescent plight, since this implies some cognition of a conflict in roles. These were children who had simply taken on the mannerisms of whichever parent played a dominant role in their lives, with little precognition or conflict about their sex. So there were effeminate boys and masculine girls, yet in no way related to those in society who take on these roles though recognition of who they are. It was a problem with which parents had difficulty coping, or perhaps, even understanding. These parents had not been helped by those in the helping professions who would look at such symptoms and see only the superficial similarities. Many parent-child relationships have been permanently damaged by consultations which have convinced them that they are responsible for their children's personality issues. Instead of finding positive ways for a parent to teach an effeminate boy how to be more effectively masculine, for example, the negative direction was taken in which the mother was advised to subdue her role.

Another child, much more aware of himself, had developed a sense of complete failure as a functioning person. His response was to retreat from becoming a social person. Added to this were his academic failures. His parents, whose expectations of him were higher, may have unwittingly created a snowballing effect. What was obvious from all this was that parents, faced with problems unique to them, had fallen back on their own resources, with little real help from outside.

The most common problem amongst us was sibling relationships. There were varying degrees of recognition of this as an area of concern. Most of the children with disabilities in the group were older than their siblings. (Statistically, this follows a typical pattern, for there are more first-born children with brain injury, with third-born being next in percentages. Our child fell into the latter category). In many cases, the problem of the younger child surpassing the older child either academically or socially set up a difficult family situation. Younger children cannot be expected to feel tolerant of an older brother or sister who has difficulty respecting their territorial possessions, or keeping pace with their cognitive and social capacities. Nor can they understand why their older brother or sister should not share equally the obligations or the attention they get as part of the family unit.

There did not seem to be any simple answers to problems like these. Some parents placed less emphasis on training their special child in order to give more time to the other siblings' training. This frequently meant taking on more than their share of chores and responsibilities for the younger children. Seeing their older sibling under less stress, it would be natural for them to feel rebellious, disdainful of him, and even a dislike for the sibling with disabilities. If the parent attempted to rationalize this treatment by explaining about the special child, this could backfire and result in a sense of shame or a low level of respect for whatever abilities his sibling did have, which could become a lifelong attitude. If, on the other hand, the parent attempted to place more emphasis on having the child with disabilities share in the responsibilities of the household, would not this require too much of her time and energies, thus denying the other children their rightful share? And would not a failure to accomplish a degree of achievement proportionate to the time invested still result in similar feelings about their brother's or sister's "uselessness"? The problem of family cooperation does not end with the household issues. It extends into every aspect of family life, whether it be pleasurable pursuits or learning activities. One child cannot share equally. His birth right is denied.

The group was to wrestle with this problem constantly, each parent coping in different ways, perhaps to his satisfaction, perhaps not; it was hard to tell. Hal and I were facing similar conflicts, though we were a little more lucky in this respect. For a long time, our older children accepted Jesse's role as the younger, and thus more helpless, brother. They even became, intuitively, a warm, loving little mama and papa to him while he was still young. Gradually, this changed as he grew older.

One day Andrew expressed his disappointment and a subtle sense of shame.

"Will Jesse ever be normal, Mommy?"

"I don't know, Andrew. We'll have to help him learn to behave more normally."

"I sure hope he 'gets better' soon."

Then there was Lynn.

"I wish I could have an older sister, Mommy."

"Why, Lynn?"

"Because it would be so much fun to play with her, and do things with her."

"Well, you can play with your brothers."

"They're no fun. Andrew plays with his model planes all the time. And Jesse doesn't understand anything."

Lynn's oft-expressed wish that she could have an older sister to emulate was not untypical of other little girls, but perhaps the feeling was a little stronger because of the mother role thrust upon her.

A consequent danger in management of this situation did not become fully apparent to me, as we discussed these things with the group, until years later. Yet it was a danger I recognized in some of the other parents' judgments. Some expressed a desire for their younger children to grow up and take over the major responsibility toward their disabled brother or sister, even going so far as to provide this in their wills. It is hard to know the wrong or right of the matter. How does one resolve the thorny questions that life will bring, such as, *who is to look after these children when the parents are no longer able to do it?* With our normal children, we can provide for their guardianship during their minority with relatives or friends. But who can one ask to undertake the burden of a child with mental, and possibly additional physical challenges, especially if such a burden may be life-long? Some parents have discovered partial answers in the sheltered workshops, half-way houses, or various group homes that exist (though far too few, even today) as life support systems. But to suppose that any such resolution can take the place of family and friends is illusory. *What's the answer? Don't die, mother, until a better solution is found.*

Whatever their feelings, it was a conscious action these parents undertook, while mine was unconsciously building toward such a resolution. The role my children assumed, by reason of their chronological ages, can unconsciously become assimilated as the natural course of events. It would be all too easy to take advantage of their good nature and begin to saddle them with too much responsibility for Jesse. It would also be too easy to expect more understanding, more patience, even more gratitude for nature's favors to them, than their maturity permitted. A delicate balance exists between the kind of sharing that creates closer family bonds, and the kind that robs family members, including the child with disabilities, of their individuality. For one can practice an inverse discrimination, in which the more vulnerable child is robbed of his dignity and respect because of too much protection. Parents must be referees in a gentle contest that everyone should win.

One question never fully explored, lying dormant but not out of the picture, was what could be called the "displacement effect". In the physical sciences, this would refer to strain caused by the blocking of a natural force of movement, resulting in displacement vectors into surrounding areas. A parent of normal children may have expectations for each of her children, if not of equal force, at least bearing some relationship to each child's abilities, which may provide sufficient outlet for the parent's energies and motivations toward her children. When average expectations are blocked toward one child, it is logical that excess waves of energy will flow out to the other children, who may have difficulty withstanding the additional current.

One can assume that these displacement waves will affect the other children's lives, how much and how damaging is difficult to assess. I cannot measure how much of my ambitions and any disappointments I may have felt in Lynn and Andrew are the result of diverted frustration. Unlike the physical sciences, one cannot quantify the outcome of normal expectations (if one can decide what is "normal expectations"), as opposed to extraordinary ones. Even being aware of these forces cannot necessarily prevent them from happening. Unfortunately, knowledge is not enough.

As Jesse grew older, other problems developed, in ways hardly touched upon in our group counseling sessions. If sibling relationships were explored, the more explosive situation of friends being exposed to the "tainted" brother or sister remained unresolved. Lynn and Andrew now in the third and fourth grades were very conscious of the cruel barbs other children could use against them. Jesse was their Achilles heel. Thrusts such as, "What are you, retarded?" struck right at the nerve, whether or not it was said with any awareness of their family situation. A wish to hide Jesse, keep him out of sight whenever their friends were over, became an obsession. This I could not permit. The pain of knowing they were ashamed of him was too much to bear (nor was it more acceptable because I had borne similar feelings during Jesse's early years). Such feelings are communicated to the child with disabilities. The other children tended to forget, or did not fully comprehend, that their younger brother, even though less expressive, might feel hurt by their actions. I explained this to them. I also told them that I would manage the situation so that Jesse would know how to behave appropriately. The intent was to use preventive medicine so that the children's friends would not be exposed to his inappropriate mannerisms, his bizarre expressions, silly questions, or the way he had of touching people. I would create, I thought, an artificial atmosphere long enough to get the children through for a short time.

Jesse liked being around other people, and always looked forward to having company at the house. He would learn the names of the children's friends and ask for them frequently. He earnestly tried to behave, at times almost succeeding. But then came the inevitable moment when he would forget and do something embarrassing. Even if the offending action was minor, it was enough to send his over-sensitive siblings' nature into a panic. One such scene, reconstructed from later reports by Lynn and Andrew went like this:

Jesse is in Lynn's room, listening to music, while she and her girlfriend play a game. He sits quietly for awhile, enjoying the music. Then he gets up and walks over to see what the girls are doing. They are throwing some dice and moving pawns on a board. Jesse wants to play, too.

"Jesse, stop that. Leave the dice alone," Lynn says. Jesse continues to hold them, sensing the sharpness in Lynn's voice.

"Jesse, if you don't put them down, I'll call Mommy and you won't stay here with us." Jesse puts the dice down and goes back to the stereo.

But the other child has been shifting her glance at Jesse, which Lynn notices.

They go on with their game. Suddenly, Lynn looks up at Jesse again.

"Stop talking to yourself," she says curtly. Jesse stops, but now the other child is frankly staring at him. He begins to rock, feeling uncomfortable and unhappy.

"Jesse, get out," Lynn yells.

Now Jesse has tears in his eyes. "Jesse be good, Lynn," he says.

"Jesse won't do it again."

But by now the embarrassment was too much for Lynn. Andrew attracted by the commotion, had come to see what was happening. They both wouldn't listen to his pleas, insisting he leave. The mole hill turned into a mountain, as everyone's attention was focused on Jesse, and Lynn felt she could never ask her friend back again.

Jesse could not handle the rebuke. Acutely aware of having somehow messed up, he now descended into all the bizarre patterns of speech and behavior he had tried to control. As I came running up the stairs, I saw him trying to pat Lynn and Andrew, sobbing, saying he's sorry, and only infuriating them further.

With his attempts at apology rejected, Jesse flew into a tantrum, scaring the children with his behavior. It was all I could do to remove him from the situation, but he was inconsolable until his siblings calmed down and told him they forgave him. It would not do for me to try and soothe him. It was Lynn and Andrew he felt he had offended and they must tell him everything was all right. Then they had to patiently explain all the things he did that bothered them, over and over as Jesse persisted in a perseverative pattern of questioning, until finally he understood. The impression would last, however, and he would pop up with a question about it for a long time afterward.

Though forever sensitive about their brother, Lynn and Andrew would survive such ordeals. Fortunately for them, most of their friends were to show a degree of acceptance that permitted them to live with the situation, if not comfortably, at least without serious setback to their social standing. Of the two, Lynn had the greater trouble adjusting to it. The status of a girl as she passes through adolescence and teenage years is such that she is governed by a more rigid code among her peers. She is more concerned about appearances than boys during these years, and more sensitive to her acceptance among the other girls. Then, too, Jesse drew more closely toward Andrew, and he to Jesse, possibly because of their male identification.

With all the discomfort it would still bring, the relationship between Jesse and his siblings was to become a happy, loving one. Jesse had developed a sweet, giving nature and would do anything for Lynn and Andrew. They, in turn, could not help but respond to his love. Sometimes, it is easy for such a situation to develop into too much giving on the part of a child like Jesse, and too much taking on the part of his siblings. When I saw this happening, I was there to inform them of what they were doing.

For the most part, watching Andrew and Jesse working together on some project, or Jesse and Lynn listening to music together, I knew what a good thing I had going for us. For the children were truly beautiful together. Jesse was to become a full-fledged participant in the family, sharing in the daily chores and in most of the pleasurable activities of family life. The big gap in Jesse's social life, however, was sorely felt whenever Lynn or Andrew ran off to a friend's home or planned a social event. If I could have had one wish then, it would be that Jesse could have done things like that, for this is most indicative of a child's later adjustment to society. The ability to get along with one's peers and to be active in the social milieu, is possibly more important to a happy adult life than all the academic knowledge put together.

What a lesson children like Jesse have to teach us today, with our predilection toward sitting around computers, TV, and other outlets that are crowding out face-to-face social communication! Many people don't realize how important an asset this is, or they would give at least as much attention to its development in their youngsters as they do to academics. It is an under-developed aspect of school life, yet education for citizenship requires the ability to reach out to others around us. We are, after all, social animals who cannot live as an entity unto ourselves. "People," as the song goes, "who need people, are the luckiest people in the world."[1]

Jesse needs people.

---

1. "People", Jules Styne, composer, Bob Merrill, Lyricist from the Broadway show "Funny Girl", 1964

10

A FORK IN THE ROAD

The college stood in quiet, dignified relief against the soft green turf of the campus grounds. Students were lounging on its inviting restfulness, laughing, munching apples, or with heads buried in their texts. The gates of the school, as I drove through them, seemed to be saying, "Enter if you dare, for within these walls live a select population of happy, carefree youth untouched by life's base realities." It was with a mixture of awe, excitement, and yet a feeling that I no longer belonged in this setting that I parked my car in the visitor's parking lot and walked to the Registrar's office.

The decision to go back to school was a long time in coming. The days of my golden youth when I'd had my first college experiences were long since over, and the passing of so many years gave me much trepidation about taking such a step. Could I still be a good student and recall study habits so long unused? The fear of failure loomed ever large. Strong motivations overcame any feelings of hesitancy. A few courses, I thought, to better understand what makes Jesse tick. But there was another reason also. For too many years I had been an outsider, on the defensive for wanting to know everything I could learn about my own son. Doctors, psychiatrists and educators had helped build this barrier. The tortures parents were encountering in trying to raise their special children owes no small measure to the lack of communication and guidance they so badly needed.

A big file of reports had grown up over the years, much of it labeled "confidential". Too technical, they would imply, so it must be "interpreted" for us. But not too technical for anyone remotely connected to special education, who was being judged more competent to read such materials than those closest to the child, the parents. In reality, the message was clear: parents were being judged too emotionally connected to the child and therefore not objective enough to have direct access. The condescension implied in keeping parents from reading reports left in its wake a quiet fury in me and new determination to conquer over this philosophy. Somehow, only parents were judged incapable of understanding the language, regardless of their intelligence, education or experience.

What is it about mothers and fathers, I wondered, that makes it so important to hold us at arm's length, to keep us in the dark about our own children? I thought about all the people along the way who had seen Jesse. The first pediatrician I had been seeing who listened to my reports on his development and had kept his diagnosis from me; the neurologist who saw Jesse for two years and in all that time could give me no positive help, not even a referral to someone else for guidance; the psychiatrists who threw out enough dire verbiage to raise fear in me but nothing else; the Grimlads who batten on our fears. All had written lengthy reports, dissecting their subject like some inanimate thing. My role had been very small in all of this, what I knew about my son of little value.

It is ironic that a parent who started off with impediments in dealing with her special child was then further impeded by the very professionals who were supposed to be enlightened and knowledgeable about improving the situation. It was never clear whether they were saying that parents were less capable than other groups of learning the meaning of terms they didn't understand, or that the subjectivity of the parent's involvement would hinder the proper understanding of the material. Yet we are no less capable intellectually and emotionally than any staff member of a bureaucracy whose reputation is on the line when he undertakes the responsibility of putting into the record, for posterity to see, a long-range diagnosis or classification affecting the entire school life of the child. Nothing could be worse for parents than this lack of knowledge about the record, and more than that, the lack of acceptance of their role it betokens. We tend to be more afraid of things we don't understand than things we do. At least when it's out in the open, we are free to discuss, to learn, to argue, even disagree, based on our own experiences with our child, and to get into the record another dimension of the total picture. The esoteric nature surrounding the procedures could only tend to further emphasize the fears we have about gaps between the child and his normal peers. To a parent whose child's future is an unknown mystery, this treatment can be devastating. Alone with the problems we face, we can become ever more isolated.

Even supposing there are good reasons not to expose us to the full brunt of the brutal words, they were, in effect, playing God with the child, for long after they picked up their sheaves of papers and locked them away in a file, we would have the continuing responsibility. And what if they were in error? Many people over the years may be unduly influenced by these menacing words. They would be labeling our children for life, or at least for his school life, setting down his limitations and boxing him in with self-fulfilling prophecies. The time when the most intensive testing takes place is early in a child's life in order to plan an educational program; yet the most that can be known at this stage is a hypothetical range of possibilities. And around an early prognosis may be set a limited educational plan, thus reinforcing their own creation.

This is not to suggest that such testing be eliminated, though it needs to be made more relevant to life experiences, but that every parent is part of the team, rebellious perhaps, emotional or rejecting even, but still a part of the team. It is hard to understand how the team of professionals could exclude the active partic- ipation of the parent and still believe they can succeed with the child. For the true test of a child's capabilities is how he behaves in the home and what the parent knows that the team doesn't about his practical relationships. The more she is part of the educational process, the more fruitful is the potential of the child.

The only way I knew to combat this exclusivity was to learn the jargon, to "infiltrate" the inner circle by becoming one of them. If it took a piece of paper saying I'm certified to know what they're thinking, then that's what I would get. This idea was only to be a partial success. For somehow, I never did get rid of the stigmatic term "parent". Yet something strange happened on the way to getting a degree. I found I had a lot to give to my fellow students, even to my professors, as well as receive. I had gained insights that could only come with experience. There was also an attraction to all youngsters who had started life with less than a fight- ing chance, for they were in so many ways like my child. Suddenly I realized that I had the makings of a very good teacher, not only because I understood this spe- cial bit of humanity, but every time I saw a child taking steps that brought him closer to fuller participation in society, I felt renewed hope for my own child. A love grew in me for all of them, with their valiant struggle and their gentle affec- tion.

Sitting there in class, among the portals of learning, I still didn't escape a per- vasive prejudice toward parents. It was as though a kind of competition existed between educator and parent over the child which, in the end, can lead to failure. In effect, the child was being segmented. I listened to students who had per- formed work in the field of special education; even to a teacher or two, saying deprecating words. They seemed to feel that their efforts were being diminished by destructive parental attitudes. They saw us as meddlers who interfered with their work—*their* work, not ours together. They saw us as not accepting of our children and our frailties as complications which added to the child's inborn dis- abilities. Perhaps they were right. If so, it was merely the fulfillment of the self- perpetuating cycle foisted on us. Starting off in bewilderment, we found little help, even less understanding within our community of peers. Then we were barred from coming to grips with the full brunt of the situation by the professional community.

With mistaken ideas of helpfulness, some of us had been told that we were complicating our children's learning difficulties, creating emotional handicaps by trying too hard to make our children into someone they can never be. Such negative attack on the problem created a consequent lack of trust between parent and professional, a dichotomy made all the more divisive by a supercilious attitude communicated to us. No one is more maligned than a mother, for she knows more about her child than anyone else but lacks the training to make use of all that she knows. Enlisted in a cooperative effort, parent and professional together, in an atmosphere free of this unnatural competition, the effects are bound to be more beneficial in the long run.

If the attitude at the college was somewhat negativistic about parents, it could not have been more positive about children. No broad, sweeping labels here to describe, categorize and stereotype my boy. Instead, the discussion was about human beings with many strengths as well as weaknesses, and how to use those strengths to compensate while remediating weaknesses. In the cold logic of educational goals, in the dedication to the belief that each child is an individual marching to a different drum beat and with his own learning style, to which the educator must become attuned, I was at last in an institutional environment where, for the first time, my child's dignity and individuality was respected.

Ironic, then, that while the best traditions of good education demand the imposing of no upward limitations, instead always striving to find new ways to extend the range of potential, that this philosophy couldn't bridge the gap between parent and professional, between the theory and the practical application. Some professionals did bridge the gap, either because of greater sensitivity through empathy, or broader abilities. To these people goes the credit for large accomplishments in the field. As for me, I will always be grateful for the deep understanding and sensitivity I acquired through those walls of learning. I was to come away with an abiding faith in education as a durable answer for mentally challenged children—not a cure, but a means of coping. That, after all, is what life is about.

Would that larger numbers of parents could have sat in on these classes, with or without prerequisite requirements, not only because an educated parent is an enlightened one, but because here, at least, in a learning environment, they could meet at the same level as professionals. Here each could confront the other with his and her knowledge and questions. Perhaps some of the misconceptions and the discrimination practiced elsewhere might have been dissipated through such meetings on common ground.

Years later, parents would fine some alleviation from prejudice through the passage of a new law opening up the books and records on every school child, whether in regular or special classes, to the perusal of parents. Apparently, many diverse parental groups had felt locked out of their children's school lives, not just the special parent, and pressure from them was to have its effects on the whole system. The new law would also permit us to remove anything we regarded as offensive to our children's best interests. Thinking back to the funny little stories that leaked out as a result of the new law, one has to chuckle about mad scrambles on the part of some district administrators to remove superfluous remarks before parents could see them. Under the new law, I would have the opportunity to see and remove the twisted ramblings of Grimlad's imagination. The greater bulk of the material, I was gratified to learn, represented the honest, if not always accurate, impressions of other professionals about a little bundle of perplexities named Jesse.

By this time, however, it would be of little consequence personally, since the years produced a good working relationship with my school team. They, and the teachers who came to know Jesse, felt little need to lean on any prior statements not borne out by present knowledge. Even present knowledge, these good people recognized, was subject to revision as the years brought new insights and new maturity. Parents' involvement, along with greater research around our special children's needs, made the atmosphere much more enlightened. The sunshine law would prove timely nevertheless, for the time was soon to come when we would feel an urgent desire to leave the state, and in our new domicile, where Jesse was not known, the records would assume greater importance.

11

STUDENT TEACHING

Under our new Director, Renee, the school was laboring mightily to do the job for which it had been formed. Its new leader, a lady of singular talents and abilities, had ambitions for the school that included making it a training ground for student teachers, nurses, clinicians and therapists working with mentally challenged children. In this way, she hoped to gain for our kids the benefit of additional services and new knowledge coming out of the colleges and universities. In this and other growth plans, Renee was to have the enduring support of the parent body, and the unending interference of county officials with competing ambitions. For now the field was expanding into new technology, teaching strategies and people seeking professional careers working with this population.

Fortunately, the school was no house of cards. If the wolf was at the door, inside reigned security for the children, a security provided by the Director and the Board working together. After Nick moved on to other positions, Jesse was to have several more good years at the school. Now he was moving on to other teachers, an important experience for him, though it was taking place in the same warm, loving milieu where the teachers knew all the children, and everyone cared. Perhaps this kind of atmosphere was unrealistic, a kind of hothouse, but it was a rather special time, too, one I will always remember. There aren't too many occasions in life when one has an opportunity to be surrounded, both at home and outside, by so many people who care about you, and it was an atmosphere in which Jesse thrived. Here he was to lose that emotional overlay which had been so destructive, that lonely sadness in which he somehow felt his differences like an albatross around his neck. It provided him with the resources that would eventually permit him to leave this small, private school and go on to a public school in another setting.

Renee was demanding of her staff and they, in turn, were intense in their efforts to help these children find their way back to public school placement. Some would make it back; for others, it might mean a group home and sheltered workshop eventually. In some cases, the children had been placed too late in their lives and there was little that could be done at this time. Always, the emphasis was on acquisition of the manners and social customs acceptable in society. The children must blend in, not stick out too much if possible, for conformity seemed to be their best hope in a society that prizes this above all. Just how demanding Renee could be, I would soon learn for myself, as the time was approaching when I would be ready to student teach, and I had selected our school as the best training ground. Completion of this internship would then qualify me for certification as a teacher of the handicapped (as it was labeled then), and I was looking forward to it.

The years spent returning to college had been rewarding and stimulating, more so than my first years at college as a teenager. I could appreciate with a new awareness born of greater maturity all that the school had to offer. My fears turned out to be groundless. Far from a decline in learning ability, I discovered, mature adults have greater ability to absorb new learning because of their experiences and background, an increased capacity to both give of their insights and utilize new knowledge creatively, making it a mutually beneficial relationship for school and students. It is in recognition of this principle, and not merely the need to upgrade training programs in an increasingly complex society, that special schools for continuing education were to spring up within many an institution of higher learning. Now, however, I was getting itchy to move out of the realm of pure academics into a more active role in which I could apply my new knowledge. I was eager to get started, and naively cocky about what I could accomplish. Nothing in my previous school experiences, however, was to prepare me for the emotionally and physically draining experience it was to be.

Renee put me to work in a class that housed the most challenging group of youngsters in the school. I could almost imagine her chuckling about this. "So you who are part of the ownership want to have your cake and eat it, too," I imagined her thinking. "Let's see how you handle this!"

Considered generally as the lowest-functioning group, it was such a heterogeneous mixture as to include the widest diversity of age and disability I had ever seen in one classroom. Yet, they had many things in common. Each of them, even the most severely disabled, was capable of learning, and as long as this was so, each deserved the best our present state of knowledge could provide. Each of them had the same needs as their normal peers, hard as it might be to fulfill these needs, and each had that special appeal that all children have over captivated adults, if only they could be reached. Sitting in the classroom in observation of their activities that first day was enough to fill me with new insecurities about my abilities. Why did Renee give me, an inexperienced new teacher, such an insuper-able task, I wondered.

I looked over the group. They ranged in age from five to fourteen. The young-est child, Bobby, was bright, but very hyperactive. I could deal with him. But another child, Johnny, was almost blind, non-verbal and destructive if not watched every minute. A third child, Meryl, was hard of hearing, severely learn-ing-impaired with almost no sensory development, and had been neglected by a system that washed its hands of her for most of her fourteen years. Still another, Tommy, had some learning strengths but was non-verbal, hyperactive and always putting dangerous objects in his mouth. Then there was a pretty little girl, Lisa, who looked and talked like a normal child. She was the most verbal child in the group, but she was emotionally disturbed and liked to hurt others. The sixth child, Sally, was also quite verbal, but talked meaningless gibberish in which an occasional phrase was recognizable. Hers was the strangest anomaly of all. With all the general knowledge and specific case histories I had studied, nothing had prepared me for this Tower of Babel. Their physical disabilities alone seemed more than I could handle. As I sat there taking notes, I knew only one thing: I must not fail, no matter what it takes. This was my greatest fear, for if I could not succeed in achieving individual goals with these children, then everything I had always believed in would go down the drain. The basic principle from which everything else proceeded, that every child has some learning potential, that no human being deserved to be given up as long as there is life and some functioning strengths with which to work, was being put to a stringent test. I knew, too, that in the end, it was me being put to a test, for I would be my most severe critic and taskmaster. I had never learned to take failure well, and the loss it would mean to my self-esteem was probably what drove me so hard in setting my goals.

And so I set about devising a completely individualized program for each child. Somehow, I must keep them working together even while they were work-ing on separate goals. The room was very small, which made containment much harder for children who were virtually ready to climb the walls. I learned about teaching techniques for the blind, speech therapy for the non-verbal, and occupa-tional therapy for a child who had never learned to care for her own daily needs or even to cross a room by herself. How many hours I was to burn the midnight oil in researching, planning, and more planning as obstacles reared their ugly heads. How good and patient was my family during that interval when I hardly had the time to meet their needs.

One thing came out of this inadvertently, a new appreciation for Jesse, who by comparison was graced with many more strengths, a blessing to us. It's not really a fair comparison, I realized, for without the resources we had been able to provide for him, Jesse, too, might have met a similar fate. But these were children who, for the most part, showed more obvious physical and mental disabilities, and thus were more vulnerable to an uncomprehending, turned off society. Their families, too, had fewer resources to meet adversity. Perhaps under similar circumstances, we also might have been bowed under by the weight of their heavier burdens.

The first thing I had to do was establish my authority. The children could not be reached without first maintaining eye contact with me. One always assumes with the average child, that when you talk to him, he will look at you. With these children, one could not make such an assumption. They would not look at me; in fact, they could not. Yet, until they did, I was not there for them. This meant I had to train their visual-sensory system at least to the level of organization that permitted them to focus on me whenever I spoke. For Johnny, with his limited vision, it meant using his superior auditory perception so that he would turn his head in the direction of my voice.

Long ago, Jesse had required this kind of training. It seemed hard to believe, for he was so much more advanced now. The job was that much harder with children who had physical as well as mental disabilities, but it could be done. The more capable children in the class could be used as helpers. This was good for them, too, particularly Lisa, who had to be taught to make better social contact with her peer group, and Bobby, who related well to adults but ignored his peers. Mercifully, I had a capable aide working with me who would follow my direction in doing group work or individual tasks. I decided also to use music, dance and crafts in my lesson schedule. So much of this medium is neglected or considered as frills in working with the more seriously disabled. When I was growing up, no one thought of these things as frills in the average elementary school class, where it was recognized as important for well-rounded development. Unfortunately, today, in many school districts across the country, music and art have been cut out of the curriculum in favor of computers and other technological devices.

Music, a much underdeveloped tool in the classroom, has long been recognized by commercial firms such as advertising agencies, as a memory device. How often we hear the jingle that advertises some product they want to sell, only to be plagued by silly words, put to a catchy tune that keeps name recognition fresh in our minds. I discovered that these children all perked up and attended when music was used, even Meryl, with her limited hearing. Some, who usually could not remember or feed back to me three words strung together, could remember a whole litany put to music.

It was a good way to begin the morning and establish contact between us and between each of them. We would sit on a rug together, and the children must say or make the motions, to music, of a greeting to each other, at which time they would shake hands and look at each other. Later this progressed into music and dance for body image development. What better way to get children with no concept of their own bodies, to see themselves as separate individuals.

It served another purpose, too, that of relaxation and relief from the strain of sitting in concentrated attention. For so many children, this form of relaxation is intuitive, and they do it during recess or at home with friends—but not our children, who must have it formally structured as part of their curriculum in order for them to participate and feel its pleasurable results. They needed to be moved into it, each one of them, until he and she begins to smile and react joyfully. Then they are ready to do it on their own.

Rolling in a sandbox, forming sculptured body images and feeling the texture of the sand, was another method of accomplishing pleasurable sensation. The motions had to be modeled in detail, having them feel it as I did, for recognition of sensations is the first order of mental organization accomplished intuitively by most toddlers. Other tasks included having the children trace each other's faces and bodies on large sheets of paper placed on the floor. The images could then be used as a lesson plan for so many other concepts, such as the differences in form and height, dressing them for seasonal changes, etc.

We made collages of pretty colored paper and shiny materials. The children had to cooperate as a group in their selection of these things, working together to some degree, and they loved their work. Would anyone, watching the glee on their faces and the industriousness they exhibited in pasting and cutting their materials, see anything but young children here, acting like any other children who enjoy this kind of work?

Individually, the children had their separate curriculum. Lisa's and Bobby's were academically geared for reading and math. Sally, who could not read, was frequently grouped with Lisa and Bobby, nevertheless, so that she could get appropriate language training and grammatical usage. She had good visual skills and might learn through picture sequences, I thought. Johnny, who had the ability to emit sound, was being taught basic consonants through the use of mirrors and sensory-motor techniques that involved all his senses in the act of emitting sounds. Constant reinforcement was necessary to keep his attention and I could only work with him for short periods of time. Yet he seemed to understand much more than he was giving, if only I could motivate him to try harder.

Meryl was learning to walk independently across a large open area to get her coat. Later she would be sent with messages to different places. She was learning to color, to dress a doll and wheel a carriage: all the things that the average pre-school girl does as a part of her self-image and that poor Meryl had never had a chance to do before now. So badly did she want these experiences that I noticed, when she came into the school in the morning, she would stand at the door, breathlessly waiting for me to send her across the room. Then she would return with mission accomplished, a genuine look of happiness on her face.

Tommy was pre-academic. He was learning some simple math which he was beginning to understand, and the names of objects, which he was encouraged to verbalize. Talking was hard for him, and he was subject to sudden violent movements; yet constant reinforcement was working for him. I must always praise, give out stars, candy if necessary; hold out inducements that meant tangible rewards at the end of a period of time, trying by this means to lengthen their attention span with longer intervals between reinforcement.

There were days when it was very discouraging. One child would come in feeling low or away in some imaginary world and unable to work, which could set off the whole class. Those were days of frustration for me, for there was nothing else I could do but set aside my programs and improvise on the spot. Not so easily done for a new teacher, particularly when the children were acting out, getting into mischief, and I sometimes felt like I had to be a human octopus.

There were little rewards for my hard work. Monitoring their progress each day, I noticed movement, a step-by-step progression. Bobby was sitting still for longer periods; the consequent achievement in learning was in turn motivating him still further in his attention span. Lisa was gaining some confidence in her ability to be helpful with other children. Sally was beginning to structure sentences of a simple nature, although longer ones still involved gibberish.

Johnny had mastered some sounds, but it was a torturous task. He had other abilities, such as being able to put forms together. This, I thought, might prove more productive in his educational program. He understood my commands; another good sign. More time must be spent getting him to follow them, I decided.

Meryl could now walk across the whole room, find the coat that was hers and put it on. She was partially dressing her doll, which I encouraged her to enjoy holding, for she had never had an object of affection and she was attending to her tasks for longer periods of time. She wanted so much to learn. Tommy nearly bowled me over one day when, looking at a film, he suddenly raised a finger, pointed to the screen and said "cloud". It was part of a concept on weather I was trying to teach the children, and he blurted it out voluntarily—this from a child whose only language had been imitative. Tiny little steps of progress, seemingly inconsequential. But I knew I must not become impatient. Each little step could build into a more complex one. I didn't know how far they would go, but I knew they must have every opportunity.

I would not limit their opportunities by teaching the basic functions only. So I took them out and taught them about the sun by having them move in and out of the shadows, picking out where they could step into the sun's rays, feel the warmth under its rays and the coolness in the shadow. I also did little experiments with earth and water and started growing plants with them. Later I was to teach them some simple concepts on ecology of animal life, taking little trips to see animals and how they live, and carry further the plant experiments into their relationship to food and nutrition. They should also learn to do a little cooking, I decided. Along with this, they might learn something about shopping, such as where to buy different items. Then there were also the lesson plans about policemen and firemen. So much to do.

Looking back on the whole experience now, I really had too much ambition for too little time. Time was needed to find additional approaches for reaching and holding their attention, more time to devote to planning their continuing programs. It was physically and emotionally exhausting to do this and carry on my own family life. Lynn and Andrew were only eight and nine years old at this time and needed much attention also. I was aware of my long-suffering husband who had his own tough day at work and needed tender, loving care (as I did) when he came home. Our philosophy as a married couple had always been that we would make it a priority to find time just for each other.

And so it was with mixed emotions that I greeted the end of my student teaching job. As I turned them back to other teachers, there was a feeling of guilt at not continuing with the job which I knew had been productive for them; guilt also in regard to my family's needs which I had had to put aside. There was a feeling of relief that I had gotten through it but mostly frustration because so much of this kind of education should have been offered to them earlier in their lives.

There would be one more time with them before parting, a farewell barbecue in my back yard as the year drew to a close.

"Come help me serve, Lisa. Remember now, Meryl is your responsibility. Make sure she puts her own coat away. And watch Tommy. Don't let him put anything in his mouth that doesn't belong there."

"Bobby, I'm pleased to see you're adding and taking away two rows of numbers. Keep up the good work." A big smile from Bobby.

"Sally, how are you doing in school? Are you talking on the telephone?"

"Oo wanna see you. Play. No go. I give you a call." A wide-eyed pleading look as she puts both arms around me.

"Meryl, give me a hug." I took her arms and put them around my neck, hugging her at the same time. This was a big improvement for her, for she had been unable to tolerate close contact before. Strange, the distorted defense her body was making to sensory deprivation. One would think she would crave close contact, but instead it frightened her. But now, she was showing signs of enjoying the embrace.

The party was over. The children were going off into cars with their teachers. As I waved goodbye, a sad feeling overcame me. Little faces peering at me from behind the closed doors of the cars, waving goodbye as the cars moved away. How would it go with them? Will other doors close on them, moving them out of the stream of life? Poor, defenseless babes. I hoped against hope for them.

I learned later that Johnny would not be returning to the school, leaving for more specialized training in another part of the country. Meryl, sorrowfully, would also leave the school because of family problems. Lisa was to prove too much for the daily bus driver to handle and had to be taken out, too.

Where are they now, I wonder, these children whose personalities somehow shone through. Wherever they are, I hope others are seeing their special qualities.

12

THE COUNTY PLAYS ITS HAND

From the day our school opened its doors, it found itself constantly fighting uphill battles with the county which required more than the usual red tape, and more than the traditional requirements for approval to receive tuition. Yet the school meekly observed every injunction, patiently applied and reapplied for every certification procedure when papers would seemingly get lost, and take with good grace new requirements and more rules that had to be followed even after we thought we had fulfilled them all. Our problems were exacerbated as information leaked out to us that district superintendents had received notices stating the non-recommendation of our school. Yet, no one from the county office had seen the school in operation. On the other hand, the new school started by Grimlad was being recommended. Was it because they felt they could control him as opposed to a body of parents, or was it because such a school of limited ambitions posed little threat to their own long-range plans? For these plans were soon to be clear.

It was clear that a notice of recommendation or non-recommendation constituted illegal and improper interference as long as the school was complying with all laws, and this became the basis for bypassing the county level to deal only with the state department of education. In fact, after a hearing, the state officials agreed to rectify the matter, and at last the school was in working condition, with children badly in need of its services entering our doors. Renee, in spite of injunctions and threats by county officers, was going out to interviews with district administrators, introducing herself so they could learn in whose hands they might entrust the children. Slowly but surely, her steadying influence was being felt. The school was gaining a good reputation among educators. Professional advisers were being sought in many related fields, and we were to achieve an eminent board of advisers to serve the school.

The change in atmosphere at Board meetings was interesting to observe. Meetings were now being conducted like any ordinary business. Decisions were being made unemotionally on the basis of facts and figures. At times, it seemed, we leaned so far over in the direction of conservatism in our school operation that one might almost forget we were talking about our own children.

Our battle scars were showing. Every detail was attended to sharply to close any possible gap regarding the lines of authority. Every expenditure had to be justified, with the financial stability of the school uppermost. It had almost become an entity separate from the children. In part, this was necessary because of the buffeting the school was taking from outside forces. In part, too, the Board was conscious of the responsibility it had undertaken to create a successful operation for future populations, as well as a model of good public relations to attract university and college personnel. But for the most part, the Board members were determined never again to let anyone make a fool of them.

Meetings were now short, dry affairs. Sheaves of papers were passed back and forth, the intonation of voices seldom went beyond a monotone: we were formally called to order, with minutes carefully recorded, and just as formally adjourned. No longer was there a need for us to prolong meetings with a trek to an all-night diner. Everyone was tired; all were anxious to go home and get on with their lives.

In the months to come, the composure of the Board was to be ruffled a little, though never to the degree of former years. Perhaps maturity explained it, perhaps the loss of energy. In any event, the county showed its hand at last with a publicity campaign and pressure on the legislature for a county-wide school of its own. It would be a large edifice they had in mind, one theoretically to serve the needs of children without placement in either public or private school, from all over the county and beyond. No expense would be spared in doing a large public relations job on parents whose children had no placement, on charitable organizations and on district administrators, to enlist their support.

Here, sadly, we were to find ourselves for the first time on the opposite side of the fence from parents who had been victimized, first by the communities which had denied their children a right to education, and then by the county, who was now to do another job on them. These were parents whose children had been diagnosed as having severe or low incidence disabilities. All their diverse needs were to be gathered together in one location within the county. For those parents who objected on the grounds that they wanted their children to remain within their own region, they were promised that this would become feasible with the use of empty buildings, church quarters or the like within their communities.

Empty promises! We had seen enough of such ventures to recognize the fallacy in their arguments. Studies which had been produced on other grand-scale operations such as this proposed school had concluded that they tend to become a dumping ground in an atmosphere that resembled institutional care, and where children receive very little of the individualized attention they need. Very few of these children made it back to their own communities according to these studies. Incipient programs, and even long-standing ones, had become extinct as competition between county supervision and local control created friction. Soon communities would pass the buck on, and that which started out as a program for low incidence disabilities would become very much broader in scope. The bureaucracy such ventures engender becomes self-perpetuating, and the interest in smaller units within the community becomes less feasible. Even the efficiency and economy that was supposed to result from such programs becomes a farce, for as they grow bigger, the expense of these programs, even poor ones, grows astronomically.

In other areas where this had been observed, the bad publicity over it had finally resulted in an attempt to decentralize, to create smaller community units, thus coming full circle back to their starting point. All this had taken years to recognize, valuable years for children whose lives had become a pawn in the bureaucracy. It was interesting to note that at the time of the proposal there was an ongoing investigation into other child care facilities of the county which had become a bureaucratic mess. Yet the same people were proposing to begin a new one.

Now it was professionals on whose side we were aligned, for they in their fields were closer to the situation and could see the dangers involved. Ah, but when have such groups proven a match for the pressure of organized parents? There was little our small group could do to dissuade those already organized for passage of the necessary law. Attempts were made to hold a public hearing for presentation of pros and cons, but the emotional investment had gone too far, and this attempt was doomed. Even the warnings of a highly-placed state official, who spoke of the folly of building more edifices, was greeted coldly and implacably.

And so it came to pass. So too, would all my fears, for within two years of its opening, the county closed in on Jesse and many others in our private school whom they had selected for relocation to a facility they wished to fill. What had happened, I wondered, to all those low-incidence disabilities for whom this was begun in the first place, children who, because they had no placement in public or private schools, were to be given the first priority? And what about those smaller regional centers they were going to establish within the children's communities? Apparently they needed to show justification for this high-cost edifice, and it is far easier to demonstrate success with higher functioning children or those who have had a good start in educational programs, than with children who haven't started at all. No matter that their targets were being uprooted from an ongoing, smooth progression of achievement. No matter if they had to change a few medical classifications in order to fulfill the qualification for placement in the county school (as they were to do with Jesse's classification). The voices of the victimized parents, their supporters, were silent now. I knew some of them, and their children were still sitting home. Did they realize who was taking the place of their children?

By the time they got around to Jesse, he had had four good years at our school. Hal and I had seen the handwriting on the wall long before this and had taken steps to remove him from what we considered a dead end. We would not fight them, though we had a very good legal basis in their arbitrary reclassification. I almost longed to do a little investigating to learn how many children there were in the county without placement, but someone else would have to do it. We were tired of uphill battles. I knew I could never bear to see Jesse put into the county school.

Perhaps we could go someplace else, I thought, someplace where the philosophy of education was a little closer to our own thinking, where I could sink peacefully into anonymity, and let Jesse get on with his own life.

In a way, Grimlad had a point when he accused me of having a symbiotic relationship to my son. Though not parasitic, as he suggested, I had been living Jesse's life for him, arranging a protective environment and fighting to make his path smoother. But if it was a position of aggressiveness, it was one I never sought and never took regarding Lynn and Andrew. The educational system in which they grew up left much to be desired, too, but we had played a more passive role there. As one of many dissatisfied parents, I had done what I could, utilizing organized parent groups to seek accommodation to our common goals, but for the most part, it was a course of moderation.

This was a role we could afford with children who had more natural resources than Jesse. We had always believed that youngsters who are to grow into well-adjusted adults must first learn to cope with some adversity. Yet, there were inner conflicts here, too, for I had perhaps been somewhat neglectful of Lynn's and Andrew's intellectual needs. Without this greater pull toward which I had gravitated, would I not have taken more opportunities to excite their curiosity and develop more of their interests, I wondered, thus closing the sad gaps left by our public schools? They, too, deserved a shot at a different philosophy of education before their public school years were over. Perhaps in a community which had more to offer in general, in which learning was thought of as an enjoyable, and not just a painful but necessary experience, innovation and creativity might be more actively encouraged. Would they have more opportunities to develop new interests, to seek answers for themselves instead of being spoon-fed, I reasoned, in a new school system which had a good reputation for providing a diversified curriculum? It seemed to me that if learning is to be a lifelong process, it is far less important to cram a lot of facts and figures into one's head, most of which will be forgotten or obsolete by the time they graduate school, than it is to develop the habits of learning and to feel the motivation for learning, for this would remain with them long afterward.

There was the hope that Jesse might need me less so that I might give more of my time to Lynn and Andrew, to Hal, to myself, and to my home, all the things I yearned for. So many hopes for our new life, our new breath of fresh air, our new chance to come out from the rut into which we had all fallen. I had worked so hard for the things in which I believed—surely I could find a community where the things in which I believe were shared by enough other people to make them a reality/

It was hard to say goodbye to people I'd known for many long years; even harder to say goodbye to the school that had nurtured my son. I left a piece of my life behind me there forever as I sat at the graduation ceremony for Jesse and other children who were also going on from there. And so, to the strains of "Land of Hope and Glory," the children marched up to the stage for their certificates. But they were a blurry vision, for my eyes were blinded by tears.

Goodbye, my darlings—good luck! Farewell, my friends—may your sorrows be small and your joys large!

13

THE END OF A CHAPTER

Moving day! After twelve long years in one small town, the only place my children knew as home, we were leaving. It was a moment of great strain for the whole family. Even the dog and cat seemed nervous. Lynn and Andrew, who were now thirteen and fourteen years old, had been on edge ever since the decision was made. They were leaving the only friends they had known, going to a new school where they were unsure of the reception they would have. Jesse, age ten, was leaving his little womb of security, his world of familiar patterns, structured routines and guaranteed success. We had been worried most about the change for Jesse after all his years in one small community and one school. Would it mean regression?

In this concern, Renee tried to assuage our fears. She felt sure Jesse was ready for it. But were we? It was hard to leave the cocoon that had served us both so well and for which we had fought so hard; yet it was a step Jesse had to take sometime, if he was to grow and develop more independent skills. A step into the unknown, and I didn't know which of us was more fearful. We were leaving the known, with all its problems, for new uncertainties.

It was to be a long time before Jesse would become accustomed to his new home and stop asking about returning to his former home and school. To him the words "never again" had little meaning. Hal was not much better. He, too, after the daily challenges and pace of a competitive business world, needed the security blanket of a peaceful, familiar environment. As for me, I was excited, but terribly nervous. An instigator of the move, the burden of responsibility for my family's happiness, I thought, rested squarely on my shoulders. What if the move was a failure? What if Jesse didn't make the adjustment, or Lynn and Andrew? Suppose the new school was to decide that Jesse didn't really fit in? For the first time in his life he was going to a public school, and I felt more helpless than ever about influencing his education. Lynn had recently become serious about her music, and had to leave the excellent, dedicated teacher who had influenced her.

Andrew was the only one with some equanimity about the move, yet even he felt disappointed at leaving before graduation and missing the ceremony he could share with friends.

I walked through the bare house for the last time. Many good years were spent here, happy, exciting, eventful years, as well as sad, traumatic times. Hal had just gone into business when we moved here, and had made a success of it. Lynn was a toddler, Andrew a baby, and Jesse not yet arrived in that day of our youthful exuberance when the world was my pearl. In this house we had watched a man walk on the moon for the first time, along with Hal's mother and father, and my parents. In this house I had gathered other people who shared my values and were active with me on school programs, political campaign strategies, our religious interests, and on and on. I felt like I had been formed as a person during the years we lived here. During these years we had lost Hal's mother. I wished she could be here now to see the new home to which we would be moving—she would have liked it, I know. Hal felt her loss very keenly.

I stopped before a mirror, still hanging on the wall, and looked at myself. Time had taken its toll. A lot more gray in my hair; the lines around my mouth were deeper, fine little wrinkles under the eyes, and funny little vertical lines between the brows—probably from frowning too much. As I thought back over the years, I realized how much I had changed in other ways, too. The soft little creature who was always looking for approbation from friends and acquaintances had a harder shell now. Probably no one would think me a softie anymore. I wondered if the people who thought of me as an efficient organizer could guess that underneath the veneer there was still a hurt little girl. How many times I wished I could crawl into a fantasized daddy's lap, cry my troubles away and be told everything is okay. I guess it's like crawling back into the womb. What a precious time of life are those years when little girls can have their tears smoothed away by their father, and their hurts with them.

I longed to do all the little feminine things I had eschewed for so many years. Other women I knew spent hours luxuriating, bathing and toning up their bodies, and in general keeping themselves looking young and pretty. The softness had been lost in the intensity of feelings. I laughed too hard at jokes and worked too hard at everything. I really wanted to learn how to relax, take things easier. Perhaps some of that special femininity had been lost along the way. I was an attractive woman I knew, yet there were none of the admiring glances I'd seen turned toward friends and acquaintances; perhaps the serious, focused attitude I usually displayed served to distance people.

Well, I told myself, there are compensations. I'm a smart lady, and people do admire me for my accomplishments. I've got a wonderful husband and I wouldn't trade him for all the admiring glances in the world. Still, it would be nice to feel young and lovely again, I thought—perhaps in my new life ...

THE NEXT CHAPTER

We found ourselves happy in our new home. Away in the country, surrounded by the beauty and serenity of nature's grandeur, it almost seemed as if I could blend in with it, put away my troublesome decisions and hibernate. It was a false security, of course, and there were already little ripples on the surface. I tried to avoid them for awhile, but I was feeling myself propelled anew into the whirlpool again. A meeting with troubled parents; consultations over Jesse's progress that left me disturbed; new decisions about Lynn's music and Andrew's school program. So much to think about, plan out for the future.

I learned new information about Jesse's condition. For the first time, a neurologist had pinpointed the area of brain damage and told me how the symptoms fit into the picture as I knew it. Frontal/parietal lobe damage, he had said, which affects cognitive functions and judgment. He was very complimentary to me about Jesse's skills and level of stability, saying that, in his experience, children like him can easily become vegetative or mentally unstable. Images of Billy, the lost Billy, came back to me.

Now there were more uncertainties, but in a way they were welcome. Better to let the future remain an open question, than to close out my hopes. How much Jesse could learn, how far he could go, would be answered another day. For now, I would take one day at a time, plan for now, and let tomorrow take care of it self.

It is a beautiful autumn day. The leaves are covering the ground, a colorful blanket of warmth for the earth below. Tomorrow the cold winds may come and sweep away its protective cover, but today the sun is warm and good.

14

REFLECTIONS

*A BRIEF RESPITE ... A PEACEFUL TIME ... HOW LONG CAN IT
LAST ...
TIME TO THINK ABOUT THE MEANING OF THINGS ...
BEFORE A NEW MOLD SETS IN ...*

*The reflections below represent reflections during a transitional phase of my
life, as recorded by me shortly after moving into my new home.*

I've cut the cords from the past, changed at least some patterns of my life. It's
good to do that once in a while. Everyone should do it, to refresh oneself—not
too often for then there are no patterns, just once in a while. Time seems to slow
down, enabling us to stop the mad pace, the unthinking modes in which we set
our paths, and ponder where we've been, where we are headed, what kind of people we are and whether that is what we want for ourselves.

The mind turns inward, and I am conscious of shutting out the world, not as
in the past to escape pain, but to facilitate serenity from within; for out there
where all is in flux we seem to lose the ability to stop and reflect.

To judge from the increasing number of new psychotherapies, new spiritual
renewals and conscience-raising groups, it is a common need; the age of self-anal-
ysis and meditation, which in other eras brought withdrawal (think of the flower
children of the '60s and the utopian communities). For in this process there is a
danger. We tend to seek small, inner circles in which we are comfortable, thrusting out the larger, more conflict-ridden outer circles, thus retreating from a world
grown so complex and fast-paced that for many it has become too painful. Even
while we physically go to work and travel amongst the outer circles, we may have
mentally shut them out. In a way, we are all children becoming more handicapped in dealing with a world moving too fast for us. Like Jesse, we create our
own private worlds.

So retreat must be temporary, lest it become all-consuming. Involvement with people and the institutions they represent becomes harder in this increasingly depersonalized technological revolution, but all the more necessary for our collective well-being. Reflection is good, for it enables us to stand apart in order to see more clearly, but the danger is in remaining apart for too long.

Thinking back to those halcyon days as a young mother, with all the bloom and vitality of youth, it almost seems as though another person lived in my body. Was it just innocent youth that made me so confident in my dreams and ideals then?

Perhaps part of the answer lies in the American climate in which I grew up, an open-class society in which social and economic mobility as a concept was spoon-fed and absorbed along with my daily vitamins. That was still a day in which Horatio Alger stories were believed, a more idealistic age when struggle meant acquiring a good life. Those were the days when I thought strength of vision alone could change the ills in society.

America is a land that reveres its mothers and loves its children. It is a good land, an encouraging place to be when one is young, in good health, and not too hungry. The goodness of motherhood is so taken for granted, in fact, that it is an American cliché.... if you don't create too many waves of non-conformity or demands for support. There is a gap between the ideal and the reality, growing wider for those who cannot blend into the present patterns of acceptance.

America as a melting pot was always a myth. A land where all races and religions can blend harmoniously, the credo says, a land where divergent philosophies and beliefs may find acceptance. In reality, we are a regional people. North and South, East and West: one can almost draw the lines that bar one sect from another, one pattern of thinking that is alien to another. Differences are what makes a democracy strong. There is a danger in too much conformity. Yet, we are strangely unaccepting of those who are different, whether the differences are physical or intellectual.

The ideal that is uniquely American has lulled us into rigid perceptions of perfection, and so we expect our leaders to be the epitome of honor and wisdom. Like those great gods, Hera and Zeus, the ancient mythology has been replaced by a modern one. And when they fail us, we are traumatized into apathy.

Our women are exhorted to be beautiful of body, our men to be strong and athletic. Our Protestant ethic demands ever more productive lives, even if the productivity results only in more conspicuous consumption. What happens to a mother who has trouble meeting these demands? What if her children don't conform to the ideals of beauty and industriousness? It is no wonder, then, that she feels stigmatized by the imperfections of a birth which precludes even the attempt at camouflage.

I think back to a bygone age when dark attics hid these imperfections. The barbarity of such treatment has been properly greeted with horror. Yet, in the hiding and camouflaging of our children's imperfections, indeed of our own, we have transferred these attics to dark corners of our mind. Even without special disabilities, we ordinary mortals may have difficulty facing our frailties. When we build ourselves spacious castles in which to live, when we brag about our achievements or our children's, when we swathe ourselves in beautiful accoutrements, are we not trying to convince ourselves as well as others that we are worthy of that uniquely American ideal? Is the ideal worthy of us; that is the question.

Roles people play … "all the world's a stage, " Shakespeare said. But roles play the people, the role governs, and we follow. In the animal kingdom this is demonstrated when one of the pack sets himself up as leader and acquires a look of invulnerability to the followers. Where no physiological differences can be observed between leader and pack, it has long been a mystery that such a role is accepted with little question. In the primitive world, one man amongst the tribe of Africans would set himself up as a witch doctor. So acceptable was this to the natives, that his spell of death on some poor victim would often result in the wished-for fatality, with no apparent cause.

George Bernard Shaw wrote a play called "Pygmalion" in which a poor beggar girl is transformed into a gracious, cultured lady and accepted into British society demonstrating that when one lives up to the expected role, one is accepted. In a series of educational experiments called "Pygmalion in the classroom," teachers were led to believe false assumptions about their pupils, and the pupils lived up to, or down to, those expectations, according to the pre-set roles of pupils in the experiments. The role of disgrace for a parent whose child cannot live up to the ideal is no imaginary one. Nor is it a product of isolated individuals who cannot cope with their problems.

Who are we, these anxious, guilt-ridden parents? We are your neighbors across the street, in the next town, across the nation. There are literally millions of us, suffering our private anguish even in the doing of our public duties, inchoate in the expression of our most private thoughts.

Look not for signs of this distress in our faces. If the two-faced coin of inferiority complex is an affect of superiority, it is the latter which is our outward face. We are assertive, even aggressive people, competent and seemingly well adjusted. And we have learned the art of camouflage.

But beneath the surface, fed intravenously, is the message from society. Our children, up to 10 years ago, were largely either ignored or given a token education.* It is no coincidence that the term "retard" or "moron" (1) is slurred out of the mouths of children and even adults, just as it is no coincidence that racial stereotypes slip out of their mouths.** Our communities, except in rare instances, still provide few of the services afforded its more fortunate members.

On the street, in the busy throngs performing dutiful activities, and even pleasurable ones, watch the mother who holds her child's hand closely, walking intently and silently ahead, looking at no one, seeking anonymity. It is the nice, normal parents and the nice, normal families, living their comfortable protected lives that unwittingly make ours a private hell. Perhaps we are envious of you; perhaps you cannot understand, having never experienced these things yourselves. We live among you; our lives touch yours every day. You are uncomfortable with our children, and we are but the reflection of you. Once in a while an honest friend admits to his discomfort and asks why. We are made more isolated and guilt-ridden even by the very people who are there to help. For in the kind words of sympathy there is often little respect for the qualitative value of our accumulated knowledge, and our aspirations are frequently treated as over-anxiety. Once in a while, a deeper empathy is found in a professional friend who will listen for the kernels of truth in a mother's words.

There are more and more of us in an expanding population ratio, as modern-day techniques of discovery are proving. At the time of this writing, it has been estimated that one percent of the population is born with mental retardation each year, either for genetic or exogenous reasons. This does not include the wide range of other mental and physical disabilities in the population for which birth figures by category are scanty. However, it has been estimated that the incidence rate for all disabilities combined was ten percent in 1970, of the population aged 0–21.(2) This estimate was up to 12.035% of all school age children from 6–19 and 6.019% of all children age 0–5, as of 1974.(3)[1]

It would appear that they should consider themselves more fortunate, and perhaps this is so, for they have more potential resources and strategies for mainstreaming their children. Yet, the severest pressures probably fall on this group of parents and they are possibly the most maligned. Theirs is a child who is frequently not recognized until he comes of school age, and sometimes not even then, when terms like "lazy" and "dumb" may be applied. However, frequently

---

1.   Currently, according to U.S. Dept. of Health figures, estimates are 8% of all children ages 5–17 and there are a total of 4.1 million children in the disability group.

the symptoms of behavioral disorder are discernible before he enters school. The child who sleeps badly, who is always getting into mischief, having tantrums, who may be late in developing, whose language is immature, and who can't get along with his peers; these are some of the symptoms that may be present. The family doctor may tell the parent that she is spoiling her child; nothing is wrong with him other than her maltreatment. Or else she may be told to leave him alone; he will outgrow it. By the time her child has reached kindergarten or first grade and the teacher is beside herself with frustration in trying to cope with a child who can't sit still and doesn't seem to learn anything, mother has built up a large barrier of defense mechanisms. When she is called to school, she feels once again that she is being blamed.

If the child is recognized as learning disabled, and increasingly, today's knowledge permits earlier identification, mother may not accept it. After all, her child looks and acts in many ways just like his normal counterparts. She has probably found a way to communicate with him. He's learned to count and perhaps can read his ABCs as well as do many activities that other children do, even if he is a bit clumsier. This parent may have a harder time coming to grips with reality than the one whose child exhibits more obvious signs, and her self-torture may continue longer, for she is subject to all of the conflicting feelings and emotions as the rest of us, but may be deluded by real or apparent similarities to the norm.

It is difficult to know which is the more unacceptable to a parent—the accusation that she has caused her child's emotional or social maladjustment, or the conclusion that the behavior is a result of prenatal or genetic factors—both are equally challenging to her equanimity. The perception of a damaged seed, or of her errors, are similar to those I wrote about in the early chapters of my book.

To assume, as some doctors have, that the child will grow out of his problems with maturation, is to complicate the problems and create new ones. Whatever the level of consciousness, children know and feel their deviance. Overlaid on his initial disabilities, then, are emotional ones which, by the time he is in school, can create havoc. The earlier the recognition, and the sooner he is treated and mother becomes educated about it, the more successful will be the results. Indeed, research has shown that much of the high school dropout problem, and even much of the juvenile delinquency which will later become the problem of the courts, is a result of non-recognition and non-treatment of such a child who has managed to slip by the professionals. No treatment, however, can be entirely successful without mother's support; therefore, no priority is greater than her education.

The opposite pole is the mother whose child has been diagnosed as having profound retardation. Here, in a mother's heart, may be found the very depths of despair. The signs of her baby's physical and mental differences are more obvious from birth, and the alternatives of keeping him at home or sending him away are laid before his parents almost before they have recovered from the initial shock. Every time she nurses her baby, or holds him, or looks at him, it is a knife's point thrust into her heart, as all the usual joyful moments of motherhood are stolen from her. To keep such a child at home when the world has given up on her baby is to live a life of prolonged grief. She will have to fend for herself with very little supportive help and training. To send him away, into the cold mausoleum of institutional care is to resign a piece of her life to a withering death. How does a mother make such a decision without devastating effect? I ask all the right-to-life groups who protest against abortions and against cutting off the life support system for a baby such as this, what do you say about the thousands who become living vegetables when any potential quality of life is cut off by the institution?

I have a loathing for large institutions that control people's lives. We are all, of course, partially controlled by large institutions, whether they be governmental, educational or industrial. But to the extent that we can walk away, and have alternative courses of action, their powers are more circumspect. The statistics have shown that, the earlier a child is placed in the care of the institution, the less his chances of survival. (1) What does that say about this relic from a medieval age!

While the rate of institutionalization for all ages, taken as a whole, remained stable for the twenty year period between 1950 and 1970, the percentage of youthful residents between ages 0–5 nearly quadrupled in this same period. (1) Society encourages a mother to make such a decision, particularly if she has limited resources to buy the services she would otherwise need. Indeed the services were hardly there for the buying during this time period. Some mothers fight against this cruel indifference to their plight. Such people have seen some quality in their children worth saving. How many of these children have been found capable of learning more than the experts thought possible can only be guessed at? But that many such children have been misdiagnosed or misjudged, is amply proved by the literature, which states: "Profound difficulty exists in determining what mental retardation means in operational terms. Problems of definition and classification … is exacerbated in the case of those medically classified." (1)

In 1971, of new patients referred to mental retardation clinics, 38% were reported as having "no retardation in measured intelligence." Combined with borderline IQ groups, this accounts for 59.4%. "Who these youths are, what they actually need, is not then really understood." (1)

Indeed, one need only talk to a cross-section of people to find someone who has a horror story to tell about such a case. Look at the thousands of shadow-figures in society's multi-storied attics. How many of these, one wonders, might have been something better than what they have become. Every once in a while, some enterprising reporter or investigative agency uncovers the hidden story of their wasted lives, and a move is made to purge the unclean linen. But slowly, the memory of what has been exposed fades, and the underlying cause for this state of affairs, as society hurries on with its fitful progress, remains intact.

The very number of these inhabitants flies in the face of statistical logic, for there is a bell-shaped curve of probability that places the number of children born with so few intact-integrities as the tiniest fraction of a percentage of the population. Merely to come through the trauma of birth requires a significant degree of mental and physical organization. This hardly accounts for the need to have large state hospitals holding lifetime residents who are older than the school-age population. Many of these are the sad reminders of an age of ignorance when we lacked the knowledge or facilities for better training. Yet, approximately a quarter-million mentally challenged youth were treated in residential care as late as 1970(1). Who sees these warehoused people? Only the attendants and an occasional relative. But behind their blank faces lies a human spark of life. They, too, have a need for the touch of other people, the chance to do something useful for themselves, and there is not one of them who would have become so vegetative under different environmental conditions.[2]

Of even more alarming importance is the birth incidence of autism spectrum disorders. Currently (as of the last study done in 2002), the Autism and Developmental Disabilities Monitoring Network has found within most sites studied, an incidence of 5.2 to 7.6 per 1,000 eight-year-old children with this disability.(4) The prevalence ranged from 3.3 per 1,000 in Alabama to 10.6 per 1,000 in New

---

2.   Author's note: The '70s were to see massive reductions in state institutions housing this population as funds from Public Law 94-142 ensured the education of all disabled children within the community setting. "Yet, despite the enormous number of citizens with retardation now receiving services in communities, there continues to be an 'institutional bias'"(3) During the '80s and '90s, institutions switched from state ownership to private ownership. Instead of large warehouses, there has been a growth of smaller institutional settings, ranging from 16 beds to 90 (3). In place of large mental institutions, however, is a large prison population of adults who are mentally challenged, attesting to our negligence in supportive treatment within the community setting.

Jersey. What will this mean in the future for the care and treatment of a condition that is becoming of epidemic proportions?

Every day in the laboratories of college psychology departments across the country, hundreds of students are doing experimental work with guinea pigs and white rats, in which they are trained to perform tasks never before in their repertoire. Are these animals more intelligent than any human being? It would almost seem we are attempting to liberate dumb animals while caging human beings—so much for human dignity.

I can remember doing this kind of experiment back in my college years, in which I trained a white rat to ring a bell for his food. Experiments have been done in which pigeons have been trained to recognize color patterns similar to those used on I.Q. tests, and to utilize this for inspection tasks on an assembly line. I can recall reading about a chimpanzee who was taught to work for tokens which he could then insert into a vending machine to buy his food. Such token economies have been set up experimentally for institutionalized people in which work never before performed has been taught.

In other experiments, children with severe retardation who did not speak or even walk have been taught to recognize verbal concepts and to ride a bike. One such experiment I read of resulted in the release of a girl with severe retardation from the institution and her placement in a special education classroom to continue her education. So I would make a proposal: let us dispose of experiments like this and leave the animals to their own world where they manage very well. Instead, let us put to use the vast energy resources of our psychology trainees and our students training for a career in education in these pits of hopelessness. The attention and the demonstration of concern alone will bring sunshine into their lives, not to mention what it may do for enriching the lives of the students themselves. It is to the credit of brave parents that their struggle for their children's rights have led to new legislation in many states mandating a day-school education for every child of school age, with no qualifications on ability. There is a long way to go before this becomes a reality in the country as a whole, but at least it's a start.

Why do we maintain institutional settings, or gather any groups of people into large centers away from the mainstream of life, whether they be people with disabilities, or the old and infirm? Is it that we can't be bothered with those who slow down our pace of life or for whom we have to provide additional services? Perhaps the there-but-for-the-grace-of-God-go-I feeling reminds us uncomfortably of our own human frailties. Our communities have increasingly become homogeneous enclaves in which we shield ourselves from the realities of life and, incidentally, from the expansion of our sensitivities. No group is less represented within our community life than children with disabilities. Recent years have seen many vocal minority groups banging at the gates, breaking down the barriers of these enclaves. But the voice of the old and infirm, or the young and infirm, is a whisper, unheard behind the more vocal and aggressive of us.

Some communities have shown recognition that it is important to keep older people amongst themselves, important not only for the aged, who thereby feel a new lease on life, but important for the community as well, for the milk of human kindness is nurtured in exposure to a rich variety of human experience. Very few of our communities have recognized the necessity of keeping our people with mental and physical challenges amongst them, particularly those who require special services. Those who are not seen cannot be understood; and so the gap widens—the attics remain deep and hidden. Yet, this population has so much to offer us. The kindness shown them is repaid with love. When treated well, they are loyal, trusting, gentle for the most part. They want to please and they measure their accomplishments by the look in our eyes.

Those who have ventured out of their shell to spend some time with our children have made a remarkable discovery. Their discomfort goes away, and they see before them just children, different perhaps, yet enough like their normal peers to relate on some level to people who are willing to accept them. They are, after all, of us and not some alien being.

Two groups of people have been most successful in dealing with our children: youngsters of high school age and the senior citizens. One may watch high school volunteers working with the children in after-school recreation programs and see a quality not reproduced anywhere else. The look of adoration in a child's eyes, the communication that passes between them even though untrained to work with the children, is indescribable. Something magic happens here. Perhaps it is that the high school youngster is still close enough in age to feel that communication; perhaps it is his naturally optimistic spirit, his idealism and the fact that he is not yet locked into a mold that precludes acceptance of differences; whatever it is, their natural abilities are to be envied.

At the other end of the scale, the aged have the wisdom of their years. They have seen much of life and learned, finally, the art of acceptance. Gentle, patient, with the time to give of their love, here again is a natural bond that draws our children to them.

So much energy to be used, and through the using, to become insightful, sensitive, broadened in perspective. So much our communities can gain ...

What happens to these children as they grow older? Then the problems multiply and inevitably become the burden of society. We are irate at the cost of welfare, whether on a state or national level. Yet the cost for these challenged people involves lifetime support. In fact, welfare represents the third largest category of expenditures for people with mental and physical challenges.[1] It has been estimated that it costs an average of $5,000 per individual per year of his life to keep him institutionalized, without accounting for capital outlay expenses or special education requirements, even when custodial and psychological services may be very poor.[3] Measure this on a lifetime basis against the cost of training during the growth years so that he may eventually support himself. Whether on welfare or in institutions, the minimum cost to society is a heavy financial one. The cost in terms of moral values and civilized progress cannot be measured.

Some attempts have been made to alleviate these problems with the establishment of half-way houses and family-size group homes, where mentally challenged people may live with the help of trained staff, and from whence they go out to jobs. In spotty sections of the country, one may find village communities that have been specifically set up to provide living and working conditions which will make our special people's lives more comfortable and dignified. These are partial answers, certainly alleviating the financial burden, for business interests who pay for their services thereby relieve the burden of the states. These answers, however, do not address the larger questions for society.

There is not enough work for adults with mental and physical challenges in an expanding industrial complex with more and more work requiring new skills, and more and more people vying for fewer unskilled or semi-skilled jobs. There are not enough vocational training programs for people with disabilities (or even for those in the mainstream not geared for college education). When they become a visible, recognized segment of their communities, only then can more satisfactory answers for mutual benefit be found. In the meantime, we are dumping them off wherever we can, and our responsibilities with them, closing our eyes to the cost in lives.

A new age is upon us. This is the age of special group action. New terms to describe self-awareness in a confusing array of theories—the inner-self through transcendental meditation or yoga, encounter groups; new separatist movements such as black power, gray power, women's lib, gay liberation; new consumer movements; new lobby groups. A hundred new categories burgeoning out in all

---

3.   author's note: In the 70's this was the situation.
      author's note: jokes about "sped" (special ed.) have replaced jokes about "morons."

directions to proclaim the distress of people crying for recognition in our head-long, largely unheeding society. It is but a symptom of the times: people who want a piece of the ideal, individuals left out in the haste for material progress. Once the pioneer spirit of rugged individualism was proclaimed in the land; now the non-conformist must seek his identity in power blocs, thus in his own say, conforming to a narrower group norm. Conformity is the way of life.

Long before many of the newly alienated found release in vociferous expression, a quieter but nonetheless desperate revolution was going on among people whose non-conformity was involuntarily thrust upon them, the parents of our "different" children. They, too, wanted a piece of the egalitarian dream. They, too, had to come out of the closet.

Leadership is borne out of unbearable distress. Today we see the results. Federal and state legislation has supported the principle, all over the land, that imperfect birth does not alienate equal rights. No Supreme Court decision was necessary; no constitutional amendment was needed to prove the obvious. New research has opened up whole new fields of special interest in mentally and physically challenged children and in the emotionally disturbed. Today there are dozens of categorical descriptions for these youngsters (some have estimated as much as 50–75), and more new classes to house their disparate needs are started each year. Colleges and universities in every part of the country have constantly expanded programs dealing with medical, educational and therapeutic approaches to our special children. The numbers of students in these fields have grown in such lopsided proportion in a short space of time as to exceed placement opportunities in communities where funds are more slowly forthcoming to initiate the necessary programs. Major computer and industrial corporations have invested in research and new technology to produce a dizzying mountain of curriculum materials and complex teaching machines for exceptional children.

Along with all of this has come both the benefits and new problems. The surge of attention in the fields of education, neurology, psychology and medicine must be a sorely-needed boon to the dispirited parent of a special child. However, it is too soon to know how much we have helped our youngsters in the long run. If the goal is normalization, we need to see how well our new tools are working. Until we have more longitudinal studies and analyses of results, we will still be working somewhat in the dark. The danger is that because of this, there are some all too ready to cut down on funds needed for continuing research and program initiatives. But for the most part, we have gone too far already for this pessimistic outlook to become pervasive. (Think of all the people we would be throwing out of work). It is, however, still a problem for smaller communities which do not have the resources of the larger ones.

The irony of this whole new interest is that, with all the information we have collected, with all the opportunities to disperse to the public at large the benefits of our new knowledge, we have instead invented a new elite class. Now mother has learned how important it is to treat her child in a special way. Now she and her child will see a whole team of people in school, for example, each of whom will specialize in a different aspect of the child's development. She will see many outside specialists as well, according to the team's referrals. The point of the whole thing is to get a complete picture of the child in order to plan an appropriate training program. In the process, however, mother is frequently the outsider. The person who knows most about her child, who frequently has developed strategies for coping which should be examined for their usefulness, is frequently not a part of the team. The new technology left out an important variable.

How often have we sat in those cold anteroom chambers, watching our children move from room to room, from one clinician to another, like some experimental animal under a microscope. What must the child feel in this strange atmosphere, and how realistic can the outcome be? At the end of the process, as we watch the eminent men and women go into conference behind closed doors, do we not feel like a prisoner before the bar, waiting for a sentence of life or death to be pronounced?

Then there are the school technicians. We have teachers who specialize in working with minimal brain dysfunction; still others in emotional disturbance. Which niche will the child fit into. There are the ancillary services: pediatric neurologists, pediatric psychiatrists and psychiatric social workers (and only a select few of these will see our special children), not to mention just plain pediatricians, psychiatrists and social workers. One can examine the multitude of therapies which abound, the special private schools that have dissected and selected their population from categories of disabilities, the special summer camps which grow ever more prolific and inventive in purpose. Each discipline sees the child from its own narrow perspective, either because of the inability to keep up with developments in other areas, or because of too intense a specialization in its own area of interest. Each has added its share of labels and categorical descriptions to a growing new vocabulary.

One wonders, if a post mortem were done on these children, could we discriminate and identify, one from the other, all the multitude of descriptors we have given them in life? And in life, after all the labels are attached, do we not see that each child is different from another, with different strengths and weaknesses that defy being lumped into any single category? If the child is an enigma to be unraveled, the path mother travels is a maze of convoluted twists and turns with seemingly no way out of the morass. If there is seldom agreement on terms between the professionals, nothing in the whole examination tells her what to do.

Later, when the reports have been collated and digested by the new elite, someone will begin to interpret, from his or her high perch, the language of the profession, for of course it is all too complex for poor mother to understand. Or perhaps they fear that the absence of parental objectivity would result in her rejection of the child. One frequently sees two diametrically opposite reactions to all this. The most destructive is what can be called the "catastrophic effect," in which the confusion she feels causes a kind of short circuit, and mother goes into a state of numbness or rejection of professionals in general. Defense mechanisms build up to protect her self. The other extreme is one of hyper-reaction. Mother becomes a dynamo of activity, reaping-in all of the special treatments that can be given to the child, demanding things be done *to* him, rather like some bizarre science-fiction implantation of brain currents to reorganize and reassemble the hapless brain cells. Like our computers, we feed in the programs and wait for their regurgitation in new forms. Fortunately, the great majority of us fall somewhere in-between the two extremes, doing whatever we reasonably can, with or without help.

Yet, while it may be easy to point a finger at professional circles, parent groups cannot escape their share of blame. We have almost as many brand names among these lobbyists and pressure groups as among any other. Each is selling his own brand to the legislatures and other public officials; each wants a piece of the pie for his own. Thus we have associations for the retarded, for the learning disabled, for the perceptually impaired, the autistic, the physically disabled, and on and on, all for the purpose of gaining funding to help one specific type of disability. Each year sees new names for new groups being formed, in an unending spiral toward infinity.

A child is a child is a child ... when will we realize this and work together!

We live in the best of times; we live in the worst of times. There has been a veritable explosion of knowledge in our times, yet like Adam and Eve confronting the forbidden apple, we have difficulty in knowing what to do with the sight. If we could but see that the trend toward greater and greater specialization is myopic, if we could but stop and retrench, we might find more generalized utilization of our knowledge. Some of our knowledge gained from studying special children has generalized over into the whole field of education. Studies of the way special children learn have taught us that all children have their own special, individual modalities through which they learn. We have not yet made use of this knowledge, however, in the average classroom.

If our special children have taught us one thing, it is that education should be geared toward relevancy, relevancy to engage children's motivation, relevancy to the times in which we live. It should be flexible, willing to switch gears, unafraid to experiment and constantly study results, for rigidity is the bane of society and exceptional children it's most obvious dropouts. As the teacher in the special classroom who comes in with a prepared program may find it necessary to completely discard it in favor of innovation, so, too, has this need been demonstrated by generations of turned-off kids: kids who don't like school, who find it irrelevant to their needs, uninteresting, painful, a bore. How do we know we've been successful, whether in the special class or the regular one? By the kids we have reached, who enjoy learning, who are moving onward toward independent thinking, actively discovering the world around them and interested in being a part of it.

Relevancy in education is not determined by testing abstract concepts alone, by treating the brain as a computer taking in programmed material, or with facts and figures which will never be used again. It is determined by a relationship between the real world and the school, one in which the student recognizes the connection and is motivated to learn. The lopsided emphasis on specialization further stratifies us. I am reminded of the tests Jesse has taken over the years tending to show a lack of initiative, the inability to make judgments: abulia, as the technical term for this phenomenon is called. "Jesse, pick out the pattern that is different. Which patterns look the same? Now look at these symbols and copy them from memory." And so on. Jesse did not fare very well on these abstract symbol tests. Yet, I am reminded of the fact that in the doing of his chores, in the new situations that crop up around his home environment, he has made more important judgments, and taken new initiatives inspired by need.

There was the vacation our family took one summer in California. In that bicentennial year of tremendous crowds, Jesse got lost twice. Once on a crowded street at Fisherman's Wharf in San Francisco, he followed some people out of a store we were in, thinking it was us. Then, unable to remember where we were, he returned to the mall from which we had just come. He had the good judgment and initiative to return to an area familiar to all of us.

The second situation occurred coming down an elevator in a large, multi-storied hotel at which we had spent a night. As the other two children got out, Jesse was a little slow in following, and the door closed on him. The petrified children called to me, and we watched as the elevator stopped at many floors on its way up to the top. We took the next elevator up, stopping at each floor at which we had observed his elevator to stop, calling out to him at each of those floors. Ah, but we should have had more confidence in Jesse, for there he was, waiting for us on the 15th floor, where our room had been. Though we had taken no precautions to tell him our room number, he apparently remembered the floor it was on as a matter of necessity.

If relevancy in education is lacking generally, then what special children get is a watered down version of the general education curriculum. Only later on, after much failure and frustration with abstract concepts, is the subject matter applied to vocationally-oriented and life experience needs. Frequently neglected completely is their social inter-relationships. At the college level, amongst special education trainees, can be seen the same myopia. We acquire the book learning, the jargon and become rather expert at regurgitation. But when we are out in the field we are complete novices again. More can be learned from working with a good master teacher and from experiencing children of many diverse needs and abilities, than from all the book learning in those cloistered halls. Yet student teaching and trainee experience in the community setting is the smallest part of the whole curriculum.

I would propose that we bring college expertise into the community in a two-pronged effort to foster more community awareness and more teacher awareness. Let us train our master teachers as models for working in the community. Let us bring parents and others in the community who will be dealing with our special children into the classroom setting to give of their expertise, thus making the community and the school together an extension of lifetime learning. Only when the school walls are truly those of the community can such an undertaking succeed in ways that benefit child and community alike.

At the time of this writing, we have seen a diminishing college enrollment because of decreased birth ratios, as well as heavier costs than most people can afford. The knee-jerk response is to curtail budgets and keep services static. Why not take instead the unused classrooms and make them a community-level training ground for adults who are then willing to contract as interns out in the community where it is needed, in the group homes and among residentially-placed people, with the goal of teaching the skills they need for a more normative environment.

Let us use the schools as a forum for discussion on educational philosophy in general. Let no one pay too much heed to those self-serving beliefs which lead to complacent theories about education or which end up limiting its place as a foundation for life. All that proves is that educators, the family and the community are not working together. It calls into question again the whole issue of relevancy.

Finally, classes on parenting skills for normal children should not fail to include discussions about exceptional children, and vice versa, for the edification of everyone. This is a job for every parent organization. No teacher in the regular classroom should be licensed without some preparation in identification and remediation of learning disabilities, just as special education teachers should be aware of the similarities as well as the differences from the norm, else we perpetuate the stratification of society, create new prejudices and solidify old ones.

The pageant of life rolls on. There are more dramas ahead, new pains, new joys: Jesse in adolescence, Jesse in manhood. Will he be all right? *Please, God, let me live to see that he is all right and never put into some dark corner.*

There are the other two children, and Hal. I feel more confidence there.

Then there's me, just me alone. My time will come when I must reflect on me, just me. Will I be happy with what I have become, or will I feel that life has passed me by?

◆   ◆   ◆

What is that shadowy figure I see—pointing a finger at me. Are those the black robes of a judge I see?

> *Will the plaintiff come before the bar of justice. You have accused society of many ills. You have made many demands of justice. Do you claim innocence for yourself? Would you, but for the accident of circumstances, be as sensitive to the plight of those whose cause you now plead? Are you less materialistic, more accepting of others whose differences you don't understand? Are you not a product of this society, and have you not done your share in creating attics? How do you plead?*

Guilty as charged.

EPILOGUE

It is more than 20 years ago since I wrote those last words of *mea culpa*. With all the turbulence and drama of those bygone years, it was yet a life only half-lived for me and my husband; it was a life just barely begun for each of my children. While I am hopefully nowhere near the close of my own life, and my children are still in the flower of their youth, it is time now to finish the account to this point in time. Time gives us opportunities for a new perspective on what transpired before, and to see something of the ways our past has influenced the present. Time has created changes in some things, but not in others.

When our family moved to Connecticut back in the seventies, we felt hopeful that we would be embarking on a new life, in which the peaceful beauty of the countryside would be matched by inner peace. At the same time, there was the anxiety of knowing that I could no longer be the centerpiece of Jesse's life as I had been before; the controller pulling the strings to create what I judged to be necessary for his progress. In essence, it is a role most parents know they have to relinquish as their children grow more independent. But Jesse wasn't like most children, or was he? I've written that he was a child like other children, needing the same things. But his inner resources couldn't be counted on in the same way as other children, to take over in his development. How could I even contemplate maintaining the intensity of my involvement unless I was to give up on my own development, the growing needs of my family, my place as my husband's companion? In the early years, our priorities are more intensely involved in child-rearing, and in giving equal attention to the differing needs of each child. Gradually, the textbooks tell us, we allow more space for our children's independent growth, turning more toward other avenues of making connections for ourselves. As if to reinforce these truths, Jesse was, for the first time in his life, moving into public school education, which meant more community control over his educational needs than ever before. My other children were showing signs of needing me more, particularly in the new environment they were encountering.

The conflicts within me reigned supreme. We may know intellectually what we have to do, but the hard part is changing patterns that have become entrenched over many years. I had become used to making things happen for Jesse. My family had adjusted to this role; indeed, what small efforts I had made

in the past toward delegating to my husband and other children roles for address-
ing Jesse's needs had not been judged successful, at least by me. After all, I was
the real expert.

At first, I made the effort to disengage. I went back to school with new resolve
to promote my own professional interests in the field of psychology. Even here, I
was not uninfluenced by Jesse. Through him I had gained a deeper understanding about mental functioning, as well as my own emotions as a mother and an
individual in my own right. So my husband Hal and I took time off to vacation
by ourselves. I became involved in school and social activities involving the lives
of my other 2 children.

Then it started again. Jesse was not doing well. He was in a regional school
that took special education students from several surrounding towns. There
appeared to be little understanding of how to teach children like him, and he was
being asked to do meaningless, repetitive tasks that underscored his tendency to
lose focus and drift off into daydreaming. So a new round of meetings began,
with teachers, administrators and parents. I was finding a new group of parents
who were as unhappy with the school program as I was.

What happened next was the perpetuation of my role as super mom: the pulling together of a special PTA composed of parents and teachers, starting an extra-
curricular recreation program for our special kids, establishing a consultation
committee to meet regularly with school officials. But in one very major way
things were different. I had the cooperation of school personnel within my own
school district. I may have been in disagreement with some of the policies I was
encountering in the special education district, but I was dealing with people with
whom I could reason and find common ground in the interest of the children's
needs. I was able to establish regular meetings with the Superintendent of Special
Education and her staff. We had teacher representation at our parent meetings,
and we weren't laboring upstream anymore. Recreation programs got started
with school cooperation. Changes were made in school curricula. Later, this
group of parents was to work with me in establishing group homes for our kids as
they were getting ready to graduate.

In the meantime, when programs in the regional school district could not
meet the needs of my son, I was encouraged by my school district to find a private school for Jesse. He was to spend the remainder of his high school years in a
private school where he received an education appropriate for his growth. Of
course, one can guess by now that I didn't stand by. I was involved here, too, but
never to the degree of my earlier experiences. Mostly, my involvement took the
form of working with state and national associations. I knew that they could be

instrumental in helping me plan for launching Jesse into a separate life apart from me.

I have said in other parts of this story that Jesse was instrumental in my own growth personally and professionally. Mine was not a comfortable existence in which I could settle back and allow events to unfold. As I came to grips with all that his care entailed, I found myself re-examining all the certainties I had believed in, to be replaced by vulnerabilities that lay buried beneath them. And so I was to struggle with existential issues such as what it means to be a mother of a difficult child, a woman with an independent voice, and a wife with torn loyalties.

I was helped in sorting this all out when I went back to school, first to become a certified teacher of the handicapped, (as it was labeled at that time), then a marriage and family therapist, finally a clinical psychologist. Each of these areas of interest parallel my personal state of growth. The teaching emphasis grew out of my need to understand my own child, and through him, to give of myself to other children like him. My next venture into marriage and family therapy grew out of my sense of the importance of family bonds and support when facing emotional crises such as mine. Finally, the seminal degree in psychology, which deals with individual personality development, symbolized the synchronization of family background and personal growth.

It is always important for professionals in any field of therapy to learn all they can about themselves, their strengths and weaknesses, their abilities and limitations, if they are to be a skillful professional resource to clients with whom they interact. With the hindsight of my educational and life experiences, I have come to understand more about myself as a person during the years I raised my children and up to the present. One of the insights I gained has to do with the role of family patterns and their influence on my reactions and development as a woman and mother.

Reflecting on these patterns takes me back to myself as a child. I came from a family in which my mother divorced when I was 4 or 5 years of age, remarried some years later and gave birth to twin girls, who were born when I was 9 years of age. I took on a role of second mother to the girls by the time I was 12 years old. Both the divorce, which in that day and age had more stigma attached to it than today, and my parental role had the effect of creating in me a sense of loneliness and of being different from the other children I encountered. It was a feeling I carried with me right into adulthood. This sense of aloneness and of being different was to resurface when I gave birth to Jesse. And so the patterns, invisible to me at the time, were to weave their influence on my attitudes about myself and my reactions, many of which have been described above in my story. I suppose if it had not been Jesse who became the instrument of my emotional re-enactment, it might have been someone or something else that might have brought me back to my unresolved issues.

On the other hand, I am also aware of the source of some of my strengths. Born of a mother who was a fighter when faced with adversity, she too had felt a similar pattern of aloneness and difference. As a child, she lost her own mother when she was very young, was raised in a community she little understood, with a stepmother who gave birth to 2 other children who received most of the parental attention. Then faced with abandonment from her husband while I was very young, she fought hard to keep me secure in a time of financial depression. I believe I owe no small measure of my determination to overcome adversity to her. Considering my mother's lack of community supports, I have often thought that I sought to redress the lack of community I felt as a child through my strong commitment toward community involvement, rather than away from it. It was part of my passion in this direction that led me to open a community therapy center.

There are, of course, the elements of individual differences in personality features and resilience that need to be taken into account, and hopefully, these played a role in keeping me from buckling under during the difficult years. Unlike my mother, I was also fortunate to have a strong bond with my husband and partner in dealing with issues presented by Jesse, as well as the other children. There is no way I can account for the greatness of the impact this had, except to feel very grateful that it was there for me. This is not to suggest that Hal and I didn't have our own difficulties and confrontations. One learns, in working with families with difficult children, that a large percentage of divorces occur because of the stresses placed on the marriage in dealing with the needs of the special child. In our situation, perhaps because of the openness with which we were able to express our feelings, the availability of opportunities for relief such as taking special time with each other as often as possible, and not least of all, the constant renewal of our bonds of affection, we were able to overcome the stresses and strains put on our marriage. (Of course, I would be remiss if I did not say that Hal and I sought personal and family counseling over the course of our lives together.)

In my work with parents and their children, I have found it helpful to help adult clients analyze their own generational patterns and couple issues, along with the individual strengths and vulnerabilities they bring to bear on the issues raised. When we understand the invisible chords that bind us, we are freer to make healthy changes in how we react and create the life we want for ourselves. There are those who believe that all is up to fate. Then there are those who believe fate is completely in their hands (frequently the naiveté of the young). I believe the truth lies somewhere between both extremes. We are to some degree the victim of fate (as for example the accident of Jesse's condition). But we can guide it and create new pathways that result in better lives.

And what of Jesse today, a strapping young man in his early forties? In physical appearance, he closely resembles his brother and father (So I guess he wasn't switched at the hospital after all.) He is good-looking, slender of build, eats healthy and works out regularly. In so many ways, he has inherited his Dad's work ethic. Jesse is happy when he is helping out his family; he dearly loves the same things as Hal—working with tools in the shed, doing gardening and landscaping. He has a super conscientiousness bordering on compulsiveness and an attitude of responsibility for himself. He is not an independent person—he will never be that. He will always need supervision, particularly in regard to traveling about and financial matters. But he can be quite responsible for himself in his everyday living situation. He can do some cooking, cleaning and taking care of his own clothes. He can read on a rudimentary level and enjoy socializing with his peers. He is a happy young man.

And what of Lynn and Andrew, and their relationship to him? Both are married, with families of their own. Both are upstanding, successful family people of whom I'm very proud. I don't know how much credit I can take, but they have turned out to be warm, caring, responsible people. Recently, I asked Andrew how he felt about Jesse when they were going through their adolescence. I learned that he had always felt protective of him, and as he said to me, he "wanted to punch someone out if I thought they were looking at Jesse the wrong way"—this from a gentle, non-aggressive young man. As for Lynn, she explained that she does not remember feeling overly embarrassed by Jesse—apparently the incident cited earlier in these pages did not make a lasting impression on her. Today, they are a loving sister and brother to him.

I remember Andrew telling me at one point when I was wearily trying to deal with inadequate living conditions in Jesse's group home: "Mom and Dad, you've done enough, now it's my turn." Then he proceeded to take over the job of finding appropriate living and working situations for Jesse. Later, as Andrew was planning his wedding, he said, "Mom and Dad, I want Jesse to be my best man!" It broke us up. When it came time for Lynn to marry, both she and her husband-to-be said to us, "We want Jesse to live with us." And so, a separate apartment was set up over their garage for Jesse.

Both children still continue to care for and about their brother. He is invited on vacations with them, and even to occasions when they are visiting with friends. Yet the giving has not been a one-way street. Jesse loves his sister and brother and would do almost anything for them. The development of humanitarian values, which are a core feature of both Lynn and Andrew's personality, is in no small measure influenced by their experiences with Jesse and others like him.

Today, though he still has his siblings' involvement in his care, Jesse lives a life of his own. He goes to work, in which he does some landscaping and assembly work, and he has a coach after work to help him continue learning self-care skills and to have social experiences with his peers.

And what of me? My life has been profoundly influenced by Jesse. The decision to go back to school, the development of my professional career, the empathic feelings I have toward parents facing child-related and couple issues, grow out of the intensity of my experiences. My decision to open a Center which has at its heart the comprehensive psychological services needed by any families facing life's stresses, is a direct outcome of these experiences. The journey has expanded my horizons in more ways than I can possibly recount.

And what of Hal? My dear husband is gone now, and I must travel the roads I face alone. But he has left me in a good place. My family, my friends, my work—all sustain me. The attics have been swept away, and fresh air has taken their place!

ENDNOTES

(1) Figures taken from the Rand Corp. study: *Services for Handicapped Youth: A Program Overview,* May, 1973; by Jas. S. Kakalik, Gary D. Brewer, et al.

(2) Figures taken from survey of Dept. of Health, Education and Welfare, Bureau Of Education for the Handicapped: *Estimated Number of Handicapped Children Served and Unserved By Type of Handicap; 1975–76*

(3) *Inventing the Feeble Mind: A History of Mental Retardation in the United States;* by James W. Trent, Jr.; Univ. of Calif. Press, 1994.

(4) Autism and Developmental Disabilities Monitoring Network, 14 Sites, United States 2002. Pub. by Department of Health and Human Services, Center for Disease Control and Prevention, Morbidity and Mortality Weekly Report, February 9, 2007 Vol. 56.

ABOUT THE AUTHOR

Laura Lustig is the mother of a child with mental and physical disabilities. She has a long history of involvement in social, educational and community affairs related to special children. She initiated several special PTAs in NJ and CT, and was a founding member of a private school in NJ. She has written many articles for regional newspapers on the needs of special children. Dr. Lustig holds a certificate as Teacher of the Handicapped, and is licensed as a Marriage and Family Therapist and Clinical Psychologist. She is the founder and President of the New Learning Therapy Center in CT where she lives and works. She can be reached at www.newlearningcenter.com

978-0-595-43442-8
0-595-43442-8

www.ingramcontent.com/pod-product-compliance
Lightning Source LLC
Chambersburg PA
CBHW051421280526
45785CB00003B/1106